ERROL FLYNN:
The Quest for an Oscar

by JAMES TURIELLO

Published in the USA by:

BEARMANOR MEDIA
P.O. BOX 71426
ALBANY, GEORGIA 31708
www.BearManorMedia.com

ISBN-10: 1-59393-695-8 (alk. paper)
ISBN-13: 978-1-59393-695-2 (alk. paper)

Printed in the United States of America.

BOOK DESIGN AND LAYOUT BY VALERIE THOMPSON

Table of Contents

Dedication

... For Ebie who took me to all the islands Errol visited and some he never made it to. How special a coincidence that Errol and Ebie share June 20th as their birthdays.

... For Jimmy III, Dawn, Patrick, Christopher, Amanda and Dougie...

... For Errol, your life both on and off the screen inspired me to be the true adventurous free spirit I became after watching Robin Hood...

... A sandy beach, the wind in my hair, the warm sun on my skin, laughter in the distance, the waves gently meeting the shore...

— ERROL FLYNN & JIM TURIELLO

Foreword

The following book is not a biography of the unique and extremely charismatic individual who became an actor even though it was not his goal in life. Errol Flynn wanted adventure and he wanted to travel around the world by sea. However, by some unique twists of fate, Errol Flynn was thrust into Hollywood. In the annals of the great actors who have graced the motion picture screen, there has never been one who embraced his first leading role with such enthusiasm, such flair, and effortless charm. Errol Flynn was Hollywood's first and only leading man who took the industry and its fans by storm with his debut in *Captain Blood*. The year was 1935, and today over 75 years later, it is still hailed as the most magnificent and thrilling sea adventure ever filmed, with a performance by the then unknown Errol Flynn that has never been duplicated. That spectacular beginning and box office success would follow Errol Flynn his entire career. Errol Flynn would be cast in all the lavish productions his movie studio, Warner Bros., would release. Even though the critics felt his success in *Captain Blood* was due in part to the subject matter and the popularity of pirate movies during the mid 1930s, Errol would soon prove everyone wrong. The very next year, 1936, Errol Flynn was the leading actor in *The Charge of the Light Brigade*. Once again Errol Flynn stole the show from a seasoned cast of characters and quickly Warner Bros. Studios realized they had a superstar on their payroll. Errol Flynn quickly found out that he had a legion of virtually millions of fans in his grasp.

In 1937 Warner Bros. wanted nothing less than to capitalize on their new found star's growing popularity. A total of four movies all with Errol Flynn as their leading man were released. It turned out that the four movies were not to become favorites of his fan base. The movies were *The Prince and the Pauper, Another Dawn, Green Light* and *The Perfect Specimen*. It was Errol Flynn's chance to fine tune his limited acting skills. In 1938 another four Errol Flynn movies were set to hit the movie palaces. It was *The Adventures of Robin Hood* that would forever cement Errol Flynn as the greatest action adventure hero of all time. If you have never had the extreme pleasure, it is suggested you seek out and draw your own conclusion on just how great Errol Flynn's performance is. It is a very rare treat for the movie fan when an actor or actress portrays a character and their performance is so right on that the viewer believes they are watching that character. Errol Flynn pulled it off in *The Adventures of Robin Hood*, but there would be no nomination for an Oscar. Errol Flynn and his performance were completely overlooked. Watch the movie and you will agree he deserved at the least a nomination and perhaps a win in the best actor category.

Errol Flynn would go on to make about forty five more movies. Some of the movies had great performances and memorable ones, but none were ever nominated. Errol Flynn crammed all those movies in less than twenty five years of his acting career then dying suddenly at the age of only fifty.

Three wives, four children and over twenty boats, fighting in foreign wars, authoring books squandering a fortune are some of his legacy. However those stories are for the other numerous books about his life. This one will convince you that Errol Flynn deserved an Academy Award, an Oscar—Errol Flynn's time has come.

Get ready for a unique journey, one that will introduce you to Errol Flynn if you are not familiar with Errol or his body of work. If you already know of him please revisit his movies and you will all be convinced the Academy of movie arts and sciences should, beyond a shadow of a doubt, bestow a posthumous Oscar to Errol Leslie Thomson Flynn. As you look at the many rare and candid photos contained in this book, it is quite evident Errol Flynn was a magnificent actor.

CHAPTER 1:
Meeting Robin Hood

"By instinct I'm an adventurer; by choice I'd like to be a writer;
by pure, unadulterated luck, I'm an actor."

Washington Heights was a section of New York City that was known for the George Washington Bridge and the Cloisters, a magnificent medieval castle overlooking the Hudson River. It was miles away from the other landmarks, the Empire State Building, the Statue of Liberty and Times Square, crossroads of the world. Washington Heights had one special distinct quality that was responsible in part for my very first contact, so to speak, with movie houses where Errol Flynn movies were shown. Within walking distance of where I lived on 183rd Street there were no less than six movie theaters, three of which were side by side on the same block. Unlike the cinema multiplexes of today, these theaters had an art deco style and façade, including my favorite place to watch a feature length movie, a balcony. The movie theaters always played two full-length motion picture features, and on some occasions even a triple header billing. As was the case in the good old days when there were cartoons and an action adventure serial playing, two of these serials would later become the inspiration for both Star Wars and Indiana Jones.

Saturdays were always set aside as a movie day, not Saturday nights, but Saturday mornings. The first feature began at 11:00 a.m., and it is to be noted our mothers always packed a lunch, most likely peanut butter and jelly sandwiches and an apple for good measure. It was a tradition that is still fresh in one's memory even after all these years. How can I ever forget the excitement of joining my friends and walking to the movie theater together, side by side? One Saturday morning as we reached the box office to purchase our tickets, a large bright colorful poster on the left side of the box office proclaimed

The Adventures of Robin Hood starring Errol Flynn. The poster had an iconic image of Errol with a bow and arrow ready to shoot whoever it was aimed at. In those days, when you entered a movie theater, all your senses were attacked at once. The familiar smell of popcorn cooking, the musty odor of a warn carpet, the dimly lit movie theater and the massive ornate curtain covering the movie screen, all surrounded by giant marble columns. As far as the audience was concerned, they had a respect, not only for other patrons, but respect for the whole experience. They came to be truly entertained. I must admit that Errol Flynn was not who I came to see this particular Saturday, it was John Derek starring in *The Adventures of Hajji Baba*. John Derek had made many cowboy movies and *The Adventures of Hajji Baba* was billed as a magnificent Arabian Nights adventure with John Derek as the lead, rescuing damsels in distress and fighting hoards of sword wielding bandits. The movie was the first one shown this particular Saturday and it most certainly delivered the goods. John Derek was perfect in his portrayal of Hajji Baba and the action was exactly as I hoped it would be. After a brief intermission, where I always purchase bon-bons, those little chocolate covered ice cream balls, the main attraction was ready to begin. A thundering unique music score engulfed the theater as the opening credits filled the screen. The music was so powerful and dynamic that it was the perfect complement to the opening scene of the outlaws in the lush green forest of Sherwood picking up a fatally shot deer. Taking a deer on the land of the king was a major crime and while it looked like doomsday for the poachers as the king's knights approached, the music reached a crescendo and Errol Flynn arrived on the scene to save the day.

This is the perfect place to make comparisons of character interpretation of the role of Robin Hood and the many actors that portrayed him. The main reason to compare these actors with Errol Flynn is not really for comparison, but to show how Errol was a superior actor, truly in a class of his own. In the 1920s it was Douglas Fairbanks Sr., as Robin Hood. He was very athletic, but lacked charisma. To be blunt, at times, it looked like he was lumbering through his scenes. More recently, Kevin Costner, Sean Connery and even Russell Crowe all failed to bring the Peter Pan like enthusiasm and vitality that Errol effortlessly managed in his portrayal, and it was evident that his vitality jumped off the screen. Errol was so athletic that even the slightest movements that he made gave the audience a sort of chill and even an animated feel. In this opening scene, as his draws back his bow with an arrow firmly grasped in his hand, the look in his eyes changes from pure diabolical terror to a whimsical jovial smile, all in the matter of only several frames. Errol's voice had a majestic ring to it and as he moved from scene to scene, it was immediately apparent that you as the viewer were becoming a captive and transported to Sherwood Forest. In fact, you felt like one of his merry men. As I sank into my seat the world around me completely vanished and, unlike in any of the movie experiences before, I was completely transported.

This version of Robin Hood was made over seventy years ago, way back in 1938, at a cost of over two million dollars. It was one of the most expensive movies of its day, but is perhaps one of the greatest adventure movies ever made. The aforementioned music score was by Erich Wolfgang Korngold and is a classical piece that stands alone and one that you will never forget. Getting back to the movie theater, the audience was now mesmerized by the action on the screen, "ohs" and "ahs" could be clearly heard throughout the theater, except when Errol was the focal point of the movie, then a deafening silence engulfed the theater. The next scene is where the audience and myself knew we were witnessing something special. Keep in mind back in the '50s, these Saturday morning adventures of young boys and girls going to the movies were being played out in all of the 48 states at that time. Now for the scene, the scene that was going to solidify everyone in the theater's instant adoration of Errol Flynn as the music score reached a deafening crescendo, the gigantic doors opened into a banquet room in the king's castle. The scene featured the banquet room and literally hundreds and hundreds of extras, consisting of soldiers, archers, chefs serving food and diners sitting at a table that stretched the length of a football field. The ceiling must have been over fifty feet high. As the camera focused on all these elements, including some of the most lavish costumes ever designed, the music score was now gently ever present. A harp, perhaps a mandolin, plucked away as you met some of the supporting cast, Basil Rathbone as Sir Guy of Gisbourne, Olivia de Havilland as Maid Marion, Montagu Love as the Bishop of Black Canons and

Ian Hunter as King Richard. All of these characters were dining and discussing the audacity of their adversary, Robin Hood. Suddenly the mood is broken by a loud resounding thump on the gigantic wooden door, two soldiers swing it open and there is Errol Flynn with a deer draped over his shoulders prancing right up to the main table. In one flowing movement, he flips the deer in front of the king as Sir Guy draws his sword, but the king hastens Sir Guy and wants to hear what Robin Hood has to say for himself. Errol breaks off a leg from one of the large turkeys on the table, sits in a chair across from the king and as he eats he taunts each and every one of them. The camera slowly shifts to the huge ornate door Robin Hood just entered from and as Errol Flynn looks over at the door he notices it is being secured shut by two of the king's soldiers. Throughout the banquet hall, other soldiers are slowly surrounding Errol and it is evident they are about to attempt to capture him. The difference between this depiction of Robin Hood and the other versions, is clearly the boldness that Robin Hood had, because everyone in the movie theater knew that Errol was alone. It was apparent that Errol was vastly outnumbered, but his gleaning smile and capricious wit stole the scene. The signal was given by Sir Guy and a lone lance pierced through the back of the ornate chair that Errol was perched in, narrowly missing his head. Keep in mind, this was only the beginning of the movie. To the amazement and delight of all the patrons in the movie theater, including myself, Errol managed to escape this seemingly impossible trap. He dashed with catlike movements, almost as if he could climb stone walls. After he reached the top of the banquet hall, he jumped off the ledge, landed on a waiting horse and rode off into Sherwood Forest disappearing into the night.

This version of Robin Hood was called *The Adventures of Robin Hood*, and if you watch one or two of the other versions I am confident you will without a doubt agree that this one is the definitive Robin Hood. It was fate that *The Adventures of Robin Hood* would introduce me to Errol Flynn even though it followed *Captain Blood*, Errol's signature movie up until this time. *Captain Blood* virtually made him an instant Hollywood star and perhaps an icon during this golden age of movies. In later years, Errol Flynn starred in a dozen or more action adventure movies that chiseled his name in the annals of action adventure movies as the greatest swashbuckler of all time.

Just imagine if you will the feeling I had as I left the movie theater that very special Saturday. As I headed home, my steps were elongated and I even took up a gate in my walk, looking from side to side as if some of the Sheriff of Nottingham's men were lurking around the corner. When I arrived home, my parents knew I had been moved by my experience earlier that day. I was very excited and wanted to know everything possible regarding Errol Flynn and his movies. In the 1950s there were no VCRs, DVRs, DVD players, or cable T.V. and the internet was decades away. The T.V. networks were composed of at best 6 different channels and most were only broadcast for a limited number of hours each day and night. I wanted to see as many Errol Flynn movies as possible but as you can see by the many limitations the 1950s afforded, my task at hand was a difficult one. Then it dawned on me; I was lucky to have an uncle who was a movie buff, his name was Uncle Hank, a name right out of that era. I called him, oh yes we did have a telephone, but cell phones were also decades removed and something right out of science fiction movies. When I was about ten-years-old, or thereabouts, Uncle Hank began taking me to a very special place, Times Square, the heart of the New York City entertainment district. Over sixty-years later and it is still virtually the same as it was back in my era, only there are even more movie theaters and Broadway shows. Times Square was a place for a young impressionable kid that gave you the feeling of being in Oz. Uncle Hank always kept up with the latest movies and his tastes were very diversified, regardless of the subject matter. He actually knew what movies would be classics long before that term was coined, and I was so fortunate to be part of the experience. We witnessed the great War of the Worlds, a monumental science fiction classic which in all aspects is much better and compelling than the modern version. One might ask how could a movie made in the 1950s, without the benefit of special effects, be better than the current version, which boasted the talents of Tom Cruise and Steven Spielberg. The answer is simple: the 1950s version was an artistic movie with outstanding character actors in supporting roles, coupled with an air of suspense. If you are familiar with *The Thing*, the John Carpenter version, you must see the original 1950s version. The two movies are very different, but you will agree the 1950s version is the superior one. Even *King Kong* made way back in the 1930s is a standalone classic that is also a much more enjoyable movie experience than the more recent version by the great modern director Peter Jackson. In the 1950s, science fiction movies were all the rage and one in particular that comes to mind is *Them*, a classic that involves giant mutated ants. True, by today's standards of sophisticated special effects the ants in this movie lumbered along and were mechanical creations, but seeing them on the big screen, in an art deco movie house most definitely made up for the lack of special effects. Imagine if you will, Tony Curtis, Kirk Douglas and Ernest Borgnine all starring in the same epic adventure, *The Vikings*, it was the second feature on a twin-bill adventure fare. The first feature was *Captain Blood*, with Errol Flynn in his first starring role. Once again, I was convinced I was witnessing something very, very special. Errol's movie was shot in black and white, while *The Vikings* was Technicolor. The verdict was in, Errol was by far the superior swashbuckler hands down; it was virtually no contest. The following weekend, I took in a horror triple header movie bonanza in my favorite Washington Heights movie theater, The Empress. If you ever wanted a movie experience that you would never forget, The Empress was the one movie theater that truly had all the majestic qualities that are sadly missing today. It had a curtain of red velvet that was several inches thick. Besides the ornate balcony there were no less than twelve personal mini-balconies, six on each side of the theater. Getting back to the triple feature; the movies were the classic horror movies that solidified Universal's position forever as the studio that produced the best horror movies of all time. The show kicked off with Boris Karloff in *Frankenstein*. I was mesmerized and quite afraid. Next up was the unique Bela Lugosi in *Dracula*. He was so good I never left my seat during the intermission attributed to fear. What could possibly top both of these chilling dramas, how could any movie follow the perfection I just witnessed? My answer came quick as the last feature would become my all-time favorite and the most chilling portrayal to ever grace the big screen, with Boris Karloff, this time as Kharis, The Mummy. I guess you must be wondering why I choose to watch a horror triple feature when I had become so impressed with Errol Flynn. The truth of the matter is that

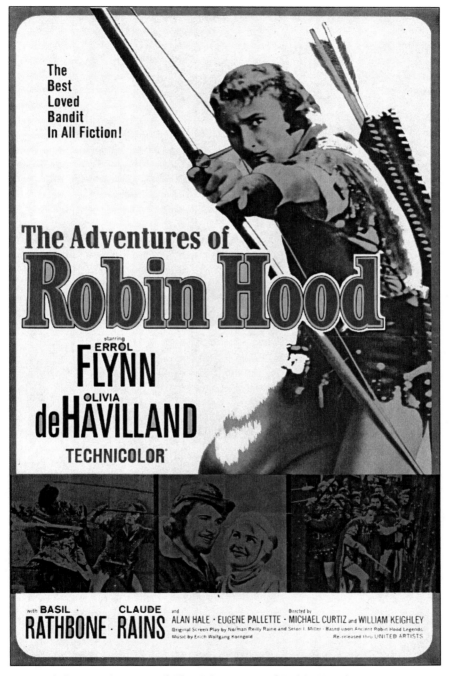

Original theatrical poster of *The Adventures of Robin Hood*

Robin Hood with a deer in the banquet hall of the king

Robin Hood with the spear piercing his chair

Patric Knowles as Will Scarlett in Robin Hood

unless you made it to Times Square, very few local movie houses such as the ones in my neighborhood ran his movies. Errol Flynn's career was rather short lived by today's standards and by the time I was able to be introduced to Robin Hood, his career had virtually ended. It came to an abrupt and sad ending as a heart attack took him from us in 1959 at the ripe old age of fifty. I have to mention the 3-D craze of the 1950s mainly because it seems every other movie today is shot in 3-D. The 3-D movies of that bygone era were very special and even though the critics might say the process was antiquated and the red and blue paper glasses cumbersome, the experience was mind blowing. The other Universal Studios classic movie monster, *The Creature from The Black Lagoon*, is perhaps one of the best examples of the technology that was the forerunner of today's craze. One other 3-D movie of the 1950s that can be considered a classic is Vincent Price in *House of Wax*. Both of these movies showcased more 3-D special effects than the new *Green Hornet* movie and Sanctum, both 2011 high-tech movies. They say you can

Ian Hunter as King Richard in Robin Hood

Robin Hood getting knighted by King Richard

King Richard, Maid Marian (Olivia de Havilland) and Robin Hood

never go back; imagine watching the aforementioned movies on the big screen and in an atmospheric setting of an ornate movie theater as opposed to sitting cramped in a multiplex having to put up with people texting and annoying cell phone calls. This Universal triple horror billing was forever etched in my memory.

Uncle Hank's favorite movie genre was the Western and he had plenty of movies and stars to choose from. Once again, the 1950s virtually cornered the market in five star Western dramas. When it came to the leading men who starred in the cowboy movies, the list is comprised of a who's who in Hollywood super stars; Humphrey Bogart, James Cagney, Robert Mitchum, Henry Fonda, Alan Ladd, just to name a few and of course the incomparable John Wayne. The genre even produced many award winning features such as *Shane, The Treasure of the Sierra Madre, The Searchers* and the Western that earned John Wayne an Oscar, *True Grit*. The Western was also one of my favorite movie genres and I was more than excited when I learned that Errol Flynn had already starred in over a half dozen of them.

Errol Flynn, Michael Curtis and Patric Knowles on the set of Robin Hood

The quintessential Robin Hood

Olivia de Havilland as Maid Marian in Robin Hood

Robin Hood with the King's deer

Errol Flynn and Patric Knowles relaxing on the set of Robin Hood

Rare candid lunch break on the set of Robin Hood

Alan Hale and Eugene Pallette in *Robin Hood*

Every aspect of going to the movies during this time period was special and most likely influenced individuals from all different walks of life in many different ways. Just remember that when you watch all the *Star Wars* movies they were most definitely based on the *Flash Gordon* serials and the Indiana Jones movies are based on Humphrey Bogart's character in *The Treasure of the Sierra Madre*, right down to the clothes Humphrey Bogart wore throughout the movie. The other unique movie trait of the era was there were so many different movie subjects and movies themselves to choose from. For example, watching Cary Grant and Douglas Fairbanks Jr. battling thousands of soldiers in *Gunga Din* is much more exciting on the big screen than on your television set. How about seeing the great Arabian Night's drama, *The Thief of Bagdad*, with Sabu in his most memorable role on the big screen? As you can see it was a special era to be lucky enough to grow up in, and I was extra lucky to have an uncle like my Uncle Hank. It was the weekend of my birthday and Uncle Hank had drummed up a special surprise, so

The hanging of Robin Hood

special that over fifty years later the memory of that day is almost like it was last year. Uncle Hank was a bit dramatic and all he said was we were going to a new movie theater. True it was in Times Square, but it was a renovated Broadway show palace. As we approached the marquee a big bright smile that a kid gets when he is most pleasantly surprised filled my cheeks; Errol Flynn in *The Charge of the Light Brigade* and *The Sea Hawk*. The posters as we entered the long walk way leading up to the area where the concession stand was located were complimented with many movie stills from the features. It is to be noted that movie stills are a long lost art form that always added to the movie experience. This is a distant memory if it is a memory at all. There were images of Errol on the deck of a majestic pirate ship and others with him riding a horse with his sword drawn. I knew this was going to be a very special birthday. To my pleasant surprise before the first feature was shown, the theater ran the coming attractions for next week's double feature. As the music filled the cavity of the huge hall I recognized Rafael Sabatini's unique score for *Captain Blood*, only because it reminded me of *Robin Hood's* music. The stars of the pirate adventure were also the same ones from *Robin Hood*, Olivia de Havilland and Basil Rathbone, cast in the same roles, Olivia as the heroine and Basil as the villain. Fifty years later I wondered what *The Pirates of the Caribbean* movies would have been like with Errol Flynn in the title role instead of Johnny Depp. I am convinced Errol would not only equal Johnny Depp as Captain Jack Sparrow, but most definitely would have eclipsed him. Errol Flynn was much more athletic than Johnny Depp and certainly possessed a unique smile that would lend itself to Captain Jack's comedic side. The most famous quality any pirate, including Jack Sparrow must have, is swagger, and there is no comparison between Johnny Depp and Errol Flynn. Add to the mix charisma and Errol wins hands down in both counts. It was time for the show to begin and the first movie starring Errol was *The Charge of the Light Brigade*, once again Olivia de Havilland was Errol's love interest and another great Hollywood leading man, David Niven received third billing. As was the case with the majority of Errol Flynn movies, it had a memorable music score this time by Max Steiner. How about a comprehensive British fort built for the production, complete with all the details of the original. This was one of those action adventure movies that had literally a cast of thousands. In this epic, Errol showed his versatility by taking over the movie right from the beginning and at least a dozen different emotions flowed throughout the production. An ordinary actor might lose his audience because of all the diversions present in a movie of this magnitude, but Errol Flynn was no ordinary actor, you were taken back by his character interpretation and believed he was Major Vickers. Many years later, I discovered that in Errol Flynn's biography he declared that *The Charge of the Light Brigade* was by far the most difficult movie he ever made. Upon reading this fact, I was reminded of how impressed I was in seeing Errol brave the sandstorms and the many scenes in the desert that looked as if they were real and not shot on some Hollywood back lot.

After the usual intermission and the habitual trip to the snack bar, a great way to stretch out, it was time for the second feature. If you have never heard any of Erich Wolfgang Korngold's music, please try to track some down, because Erich's soundtracks are by far the best to come out of Hollywood's golden era. The critics of the day were usually very hard on their reviews of all of Errol Flynn's movies, but for some reason, even today, they literally loved everything about *The Sea Hawk*. I had no idea what I was about to witness would change my movie going experience once again for the rest of my life. Think if you will, it is 2011 and Hollywood is going to make a pirate movie without the use of special effects, a movie like the current *Pirates of the Caribbean*. The studio Warner Bros. sank almost two million dollars into the production of *The Sea Hawk*. Today that would be about one hundred and twenty million dollars, but without special effects. What they produced with the help of Errol Flynn is the definitive pirate movie. *The Adventures of Robin Hood* is no doubt the greatest action adventure movie of all time, but *The Sea Hawk* is the greatest pirate epic of all time. Even though Olivia de Havilland was absent from the cast this time around, Brenda Marshall as Errol's love interest proved that whoever played opposite Errol in a romantic lead brought out the chemistry Errol had with any woman that never failed. At the end of the movie, I sat motionless wondering how I could somehow get on a pirate ship, or make my way to the desert. Today as I remember these two movies and *The Adventures of Robin Hood*, I wonder how an actor who starred in all three movies was never recognized by his profession. I have watched literally thousands and thousands of movies and Errol Flynn's version of *Robin Hood* is the best action adventure movie of all time and *The Sea Hawk* is hands down the greatest pirate movie of all time, both because the star was Errol Flynn. He proved himself in both movies to be unique, but there would be no recognition for Errol Flynn. As a young, naive boy, I knew Errol

Flynn was the greatest actor of all time, as an experienced movie devotee I still know Errol Flynn is the greatest actor of all time. Recently during a Golden Globes presentation, the 2011 version, Robert DeNiro was presented with an award for being the greatest living actor. They proceeded to show clips from his most memorable roles; I must admit *Raging Bull* and The Godfather, Part II and *Taxi Driver* definitely warrant the accolades, but the other roles he portrayed were a cookie cutter of the same character. The time for a re-evaluation of the works of Errol Flynn is now, his body of work and natural acting style has never been duplicated, not to mention the unique screen presence and physical attraction he produced every time he made a movie.

CHAPTER 2:
Investigating Errol Flynn—The Myth

"The public has always expected me to be a playboy,
and a decent chap never lets his public down."

The year was 1959, only three years after I was first introduced to the magical experience Errol Flynn brought to the screen, 1959 was the year Errol Flynn died. It was a very sad moment for his many fans, but the loss of Errol was magnified by the fact that he was only 50-years-old. If you had hoped to read more about Errol like I did it would be some time in the distant future, because books about his life and adventures had not been published. Faced with the task of gathering as much information as I could about his movies that I didn't get to see, or facts about his life, I was relegated to only one viable source, movie magazines. Remember there was no internet and even the local libraries had limited resource material on most entertainment personalities. As luck would have it, Errol Flynn made it to the cover of one of the most famous news magazines of the era, *Life*. It was a very large format magazine and the biggest on the newsstands, three times the size of, say *People* magazine. The library never acquired a copy of that particular issue, but the lady at the front desk let me borrow her copy. The magazine was loaded with many outstanding photographs of Errol and an extra informative article that began with Errol's childhood. To my surprise Errol was not born in the United States, it was the seaport town of the British Commonwealth, Hobart, Tasmania, that had the distinction. The year was 1909 and the date of his birth was June 20th. His name was one of Irish descent, but the fact of the matter was, Errol was a full blooded Australian. In the article, Errol's mother described him as a very nasty and very bad little boy, they never ever got along, but Errol greatly respected his father and it was a known fact that Errol idolized the senior Flynn. His father, however, knew there was little or no chance of Errol following in his footsteps. Errol's father was not only a distinguished professor, but a renowned marine biologist. Even though Errol's father managed to get him enrolled in many of the finest schools in both England and Australia, Errol was expelled from most of them. While Errol went from school to school, his rebellious and nonconforming nature developed, but at the same time his love for sports became evident. It was a key factor in Errol's ability to escape what might have been a tragic life instead of a successful one. Errol excelled in sports. Another trait that followed Errol most of his fifty years was restlessness. It manifested itself when he left Sydney and went to New Guinea to enroll as a cadet in the government service. Errol quickly became bored with this venture and after only a few months he began work as an overseer at a copra plantation. Several months later, Errol left that job and went into a partnership running a small charter schooner. As with all his previous endeavors to date, this one met the same fate. Bored again Errol sold his interest and decided to mine gold. In a very short time, gold mining was added to the growing list of Errol Flynn adventures. If you are keeping track there have been quite a few interesting careers, all ending the same way for Errol, and he was only twenty-years-old.

The year was 1930, it was early January when Errol returned to Sydney and decided to purchase a fifty-year old ship named *Arop*, but Errol re-christened it the *Sirocco*. As crazy as some of the wild adventures Errol would later portray on the big screen, he decided with three friends to sail to New Guinea. This ship was very old and the route to New Guinea went through the very dangerous waters of The Great Barrier Reef. The voyage took over seven danger-filled months, and many years later Errol wrote his first book, *Beam Ends*, an account of that unique journey. When Errol returned once again to Sydney, he became a writer for a local paper. Almost as if a chance of a lifetime would bestow itself on Errol, a very famous Australian director stumbled across some photographs of Errol that were published in the newspaper Errol worked for, the *Sydney Bulletin*. It was this twist of fate and perhaps some luck thrown in for good measure that the man, Charles Chauvel was looking for an actor to star in his production, *In the Wake of the Bounty*. An even

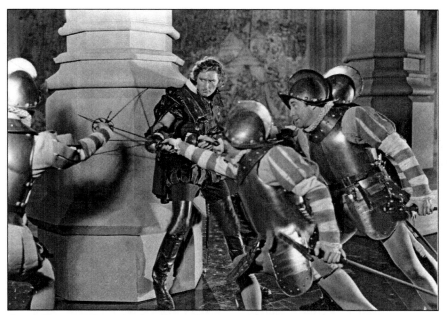

Errol Flynn as Captain Geoffrey Thorpe in *The Sea Hawk*

Flora Robson as Queen Elizabeth in *The Sea Hawk*

Brenda Marshall as Donna Maria in *The Sea Hawk*

Alan Hale and extras in *The Sea Hawk*

Crew of *The Sea Hawk*

Olivia de Havilland in *Captain Blood*

Olivia de Havilland in *The Charge of The Light Brigade*

stranger fact is that Errol Flynn had never given the slightest inclination of being an actor. Errol considered himself as being a true man of the world, an adventurer. He felt that the world was one big adventure and he had planned to see and do it all. The movie was a semi-documentary and Errol was cast in the role of Fletcher Christian. Even though it was titled, *In The Wake of the Bounty*, most of the film was like a travel log and not even close to a full length feature. When shooting on the movie was complete, Errol was completely convinced that being an actor was the profession he would settle on.

The Charge of The Light Brigade

Anna Neagle in *Let's Make Up*—1955 and Errol still looks good

Sante Fe Trail with Ronald Reagan and William Lundigan

Once again with his first movie role under his belt, Errol took off on another adventure, this time it was London. It was now 1933 and Errol tried to land acting roles at the major studios in London, all with no success. Finally, when he had almost packed it in the quest to be an actor, a local Repertory Company in Northampton gave him a chance. This opportunity to work in the acting profession helped Errol develop an understanding of the movie business. It did however pay off, because after about a year and a half at the Repertory Company Errol was offered a leading role, that's right, a leading role from Warner Bros. Teddington Studios. In the 1930s, the studios produced a series of films that were called quota films. The movie Errol was cast in the leading role was *Murder at Monte Carlo*, one such quota film. My research uncovered how a virtually unknown actor, an actor with little or no experience was able to land a leading role at a major movie studio. The answer may or may not surprise you, depending on how familiar you might be with Errol Flynn. While Errol was working at night with the Repertory Company, he spent his days going to major studios, most of the time uninvited. It was Errol's charming personality and persistence that enabled him to arrange interviews with the studio bosses. The studio head at Warner Bros. in Teddington, Irving Asher was also the managing director

Olivia de Havilland in Dodge City

Dodge City close up

and he virtually called all the shots for Warner Bros. in the States. Mr. Asher was so impressed with Errol's physical attributes, as well as, Errol's unique personality that he signed Errol to a contract with Warner Bros. without ever seeing Errol act. As a matter of fact, Irving Asher never even bothered to give Errol the traditional screen test. The events that soon followed can only be described with the term, "A Star is Born." In October of 1934, Irving Asher sent a cable to Warner Bros. Studios in Burbank California, it read: "I signed today a seven year contract to a twenty-five year old lad who

Alan Hale, Errol Flynn's best friend, in *Dodge City*

The happy couple in *Dodge City*

Bruce Cabot in *Dodge City*

Alan Hale, Victor Jory and Errol Flynn in *Dodge City*

A very young looking Olivia de Havilland in *Dodge City*

A candid picture from *Dodge City*

Olivia de Havilland in *Dodge City*

Alan Hale and Errol Flynn ready for action in *Dodge City*

Olivia de Havilland in *They Died with Their Boots On*

Olivia and Errol ready for a kiss in *They Died with Their Boots On*

Donald Crisp in *The Private Lives of Elizabeth and Essex*

The Earl of Essex confirms that Errol could wear any costume and look regal

Errol Flynn as Renzo in *Crossed Swords*, 1954

Renzo in *Crossed Swords*

Rossana Rory in *The Big Boodle*, 1957

Alan Hale in *The Sea Hawk*, 1940

Captain Peter Blood

Captain Peter Blood addresses his crew

They Died With Their Boots On, 1941

Objective Burma, 1945

The Charge of The Light Brigade

Footsteps in The Dark, 1941

The Private Lives of Elizabeth and Essex portrait

Donald Crisp in *The Charge of The Light Brigade*

Alan Hale in a street scene in *Dodge City*

is the best picture actor I have ever seen; I guarantee he is a real find." Well Irving Asher was one of the most highly regarded executives Warner Bros. had in England, and the folks in Hollywood soon found out that Mr. Asher was spot on in his evaluation of Errol. I can only add that not only was Irving Asher spot on with his evaluation of Errol, but it was Errol who was spot on with his most important performance to date, his interview with the Warner Bros. executive. It is to be noted that after two more very minor movie roles, *The Case of the Curious Bride*, and *Don't Bet on Blondes*, Errol was jettisoned into major stardom, with his starring role in *Captain Blood*.

It all reads like the plot or script of a rags-to-riches Hollywood movie. Errol Flynn was an ordinary guy from a remote location, Hobart, Tazmania. He was hell bent on seeing the entire world. His personality, albeit charming, was overshadowed with his seemingly bored nature. To add to the mix, Errol Flynn absolutely never had any aspirations of being an actor. However, the most influential executive of Hollywood's biggest, if not *the* biggest, studio, Warner Bros., proclaimed that Errol Flynn was by far the best leading movie actor he had ever come across. It is here in Errol's journey that the quest for an Oscar truly began, even though Errol Flynn was completely unaware of that fact.

An argument can be made, even at this early junction, that if Mr. Irwin Asher was only fifty percent correct in his evaluation of Errol's acting ability, Errol was destined for stardom and extremely talented. As it turned out, Mr. Irwin Asher was, in fact, one hundred percent correct, because *Captain Blood* was hailed as a great movie. Errol Flynn's performance established him as Hollywood's newest leading man.

CHAPTER 3:
A Star Is Born

*"I allow myself to be understood as a colorful
fragment in a drab world."*

The year was 1935 and Warner Bros. were looking for a movie to
ride the coattails of success that both *The Count of Monte Cristo*
and *Treasure Island* had. Hollywood was growing faster than any
corporation in the entire world and Warner Bros. purchased the
Vitagraph Company, a much smaller movie studio, but one with some
exciting properties. In 1923, the Vitagraph Company produced an
elaborate pirate saga for its time, Rafael Sabatini's *Captain Blood*.
One of the Warner brothers, Jack, wanted to do a re-make and
requested his top director, Michael Curtiz, to take over the production.
As fate would have it, this was the same Michael Curtiz who had
used the then virtually unknown Errol Flynn in his production of
The Case of the Curious Bride. Jack Warner was so impressed with
Errol Flynn in that movie that he also requested Curtiz to give Errol
a screen test for the lead role in *Captain Blood*. The screen test was
a short one and when Curtiz reviewed it the same evening Errol
tested, he immediately called Jack Warner and told him: "Errol has
the part hands down." Hollywood had many top actors who would
have loved a shot at such a great role, coupled with the lavish
production everyone knew Warner Bros. would create, it was a highly
sought after chance. Even though Errol had a very limited acting
resume and limited experience on the big screen, both Jack L. Warner
and Michael Curtiz were completely convinced he was going to win
over the audience. Were they ever correct, were they ever more on
the money. Errol Flynn conveyed a professionalism they had never
witnessed before, and most likely would never come across again.
This "Errol Flynn chap" as Jack Warner referred to him early on in
their relationship, had a unique style, always 100% believable and

his natural demeanor came across perfect. Errol was acting, but he was just being Errol, he was having fun on the sets, and not only did he win over the audience, but Errol Flynn won over the critics. *Captain Blood* opened in December 1935 and all the reviews of this brand new swashbuckling super star in the making far exceeded all of Warner Bros.' expectations. Today the studios are not overly concerned with the reviews that are given to their movies, because unlike the golden age, a movie's success today is based almost entirely on promotion. In 1935, the reviews were the greatest aspect that all the major studios worked for, but the box office success coupled with a great review Errol Flynn received, cemented Errol immediately as a major motion picture star. Even though *Captain Blood* was made over 75 years ago, it still holds up as a one of the greatest pirate movies ever made. One of the aspects of the production that also is timeless involves the character of Peter Blood. It was so masterfully crafted by Errol Flynn in his very first blockbuster movie. It was also the very first time Errol was fortunate enough to have Olivia de Havilland as his co-star; and the two great actors teamed up to make seven additional movies. Erich Wolfgang Korngold composed the original film score, also his first, and he would work with Errol on six more movies. Michael Curtiz who was regarded as one of Hollywood's greatest directors enjoyed working with Errol on *Captain Blood*, and they teamed up eight more times. However, near the end of their working relationship they developed a friction that ultimately ended this great pairing of two very talented personalities. It should also be noted that *Captain Blood* had one of the most successful runs of any motion picture throughout the world. *Captain Blood* was so popular that Warner Bros. re-released it every few years to take advantage of the fact that the movie would always appeal to new generations of movie fans. It was that practice that Warner Bros. used, the re-release program that enabled my generation the ability to see older movie classics from the Warner Bros.' catalog. In today's environment there are numerous ways to catch older movies one might have missed, for example DVD's and cable television are the two most common venues.

Errol Flynn was like a snowball rolling down a mountain after the immediate success of *Captain Blood*. Everything happened so fast Errol never had a chance to look back at the beginning. It

Errol takes a break on the set of _Adventures of Captain Fabian_

would be a decade later before Errol realized the adventure he so longed for off the screen was robbed from him by the adventures he was acting out on the screen. In the 1940s and 1950s all the big Hollywood stars were really thought of as being much bigger than life and in the case of Errol it was more than that. As soon as Errol realized his love of the ocean and the tropical islands of the Caribbean he longed for were a distant memory. He became a restless

Captain Fabian in action

Relaxing on set

soul off the back-lot movie sets. His energy now focused on physical tasks such as fencing and tennis. Most of the stunts in his movies were performed by Errol himself and while making *Captain Blood*, Errol became so good at fencing that by the end of the production Errol was much more masterful than his instructors. In Beverly Hills, some of the finest tennis pros were usually no match for Errol, and if he had wanted to be a tennis professional, he most certainly would have been highly successful.

Taking a break with man's best friend

Shirtless on set writing a book perhaps?

Errol contemplating his next move

Errol and Patrice Wymore on the set of *Rocky Mountain*

A happy Errol Flynn

Errol giving and autograph to somebody

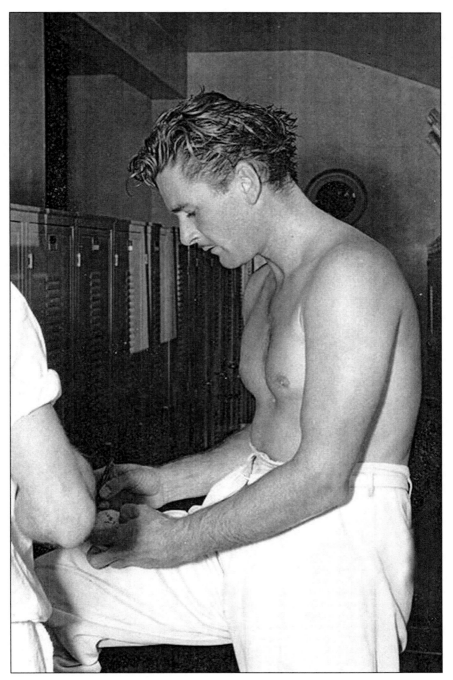

Errol signing a cricket ball

Errol in his element

Dapper looking Errol

Candid shot of Errol in the shower, always smiling

A day at the races

Bette Davis and Errol Flynn

Errol and his pal

Say cheese!

Taking a break

A girl on each arm

Errol and Gina Lollobridgida in *Crossed Swords*

Relaxing with Patrice Wymore on the set of *Rocky Mountain*

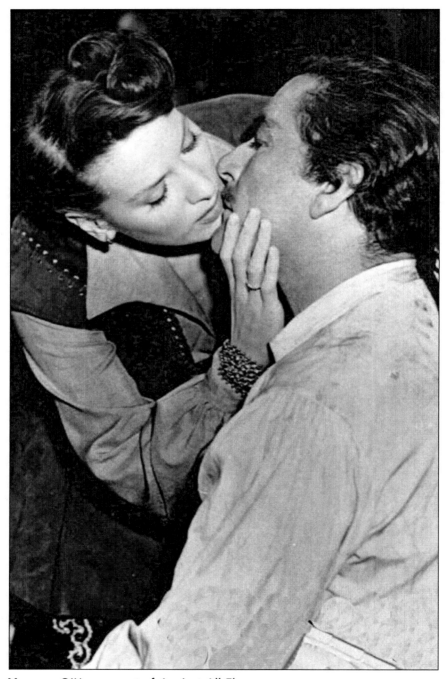

Maureen O'Hara on set of *Against All Flags*

A close up of Errol in *The Private Lives of Elizabeth and Essex*

Left and Above: Publicity photos

Left and Above: Publicity photos

Left and Above: Publicity photos

Left and Above: Publicity photos

A candid picture of Errol Flynn in 1956

Publicity photo

Left and Above: Publicity photos

Left and Above: Publicity photos

Warner Bros. was never known for being frugal with its top stars and Errol was highly compensated for his role in *Captain Blood*. Try to imagine, if you will, the fact that Errol Flynn was only in his mid-twenties, had just starred in one of the most successful movies Warner Bros. had ever produced, and he was the most charismatic male actors in all of Hollywood. The empty pockets Errol was always used to carrying around were now filled with plenty of cash. It led to the next phase in Errol's Hollywood saga, namely young beautiful starlets. It is my belief, based on my research into the life of Errol Flynn, that Lili Damita, Errol's first wife, would prove to lead to his demise. Most, if not all of the autobiographies omit the fact that Errol met Lili for the very first time on the boat that brought them to America in 1934. It appears that Lili, a French actress who was several years older than Errol, decided this was her chance to rope in the big catch. Another important fact omitted is that Lili had been married a decade before to the same director, Michael Curtiz, who made *Captain Blood*. Her marriage to Michael Curtiz lasted less than a year. I doubt that Errol was aware of Lili's past. Everything was coming at him much too fast. Lili wasted no time, and she managed to marry Errol in 1935, the only positive that came out of the tumultuous relationship was Errol's only son, Sean. Lili and Errol were two of Hollywood's most photographed couples and also the couple that the gossip columnists always had something juicy to write about. In 1942, the couple called it quits, but right until his death in 1959, Lili had always managed to be a thorn in Errol's side.

The die had been cast with the success of *Captain Blood*, and Warner Bros. Studios had a whole list of movies lined up to specifically showcase their brand new superstar property. I was very surprised that in the next ten movies that Errol Flynn starred in after *Captain Blood*, only two of those movies could be categorized in the action adventure genre. First on the list was *The Charge of the Light Brigade*, then after a couple of dramas, Errol was cast as Robin Hood, in *The Adventures of Robin Hood*. If you look at *The Dawn Patrol* and *Another Dawn*, both of these movies lacked the action scenes that would put them in the action adventure genre of movies Errol made during this phase of his career. Both of those movies were good solid war dramas, but without the star power Errol generated probably would have been failures. It would be almost a decade later before Errol would return to the roles he was always more comfortable and suited for.

CHAPTER 4:
Move over Clint...

"My job is to defy the normal."

In Hollywood, everyone was talking about the brand new superstar. Every beautiful young starlet wanted to meet him, for that matter even the older ones wanted him. Riding on the success of *Captain Blood, The Charge of the Light Brigade* and *The Adventures of Robin Hood,* Warner Bros. had another well thought-out plan in the works for Errol, star Errol in Westerns. When people think of the greatest Western movie actors of all time many names come to mind, John Wayne and Clint Eastwood probably top the list, but Alan Ladd, Henry Fonda and James Stewart could be included. Errol Flynn should be near the top of the list but is most likely omitted. If you wish to make your own comparison you can pick up a box set of Errol Flynn Westerns and decide for yourself. I am confident Errol will impress you once again with his ability to play a Western hero as good, if not better than all the actors before or after him. The year was 1939, and Warner Bros. decided to promote Errol's first Western, *Dodge City* more than any of their 1939 productions. The powers that be at Warner Bros. Studios had no idea that Errol Flynn was once again a big hit, not only at the box office, but with the critics as well. The recipe once again was comprised of the great director, Michael Curtiz, Errol's favorite leading lady, Olivia de Havilland, and a rousing, if not truly magnificent music score by Max Steiner. Even today reviews state that the movie has every element the avid Western movie fan would hope to find in a Western, but this one also had Errol Flynn as its star. Errol went on to make several other Western movies. The list is a formidable one and includes, *Virginia City, Silver River, Montana, Rocky Mountain* and *The Santa Fe Trail.* One more Western Errol Flynn starred in was *They Died with Their Boots On* which was made in 1941. It is the definitive Western that defines Errol as one of Hollywood's greatest leading men. It seemed whenever Errol Flynn made a blockbuster movie, he was always joined by a bunch of familiar characters. Olivia de Havilland played Errol's leading lady once again and Max Steiner added his blend of a truly moving music score. Raoul Walsh was the director this time around and he proved to be a formidable choice and an equal to Michael Curtiz. There was a new up and coming actor named Anthony Quinn, who was perfect as the leader of the Lakota Indians, Chief Crazy Horse. *They Died with Their Boots On* was one of the top grossing movies of 1941. Errol was bringing in the most revenue to the Warner Bros. Studios, more than any of their other actors. I am convinced that Warner Bros. were satisfied with all the box office results their star, Errol Flynn, delivered. However, on the other hand, I feel they lost focus on the artistic value these movies contained. *They Died with Their Boots On* is a virtual masterpiece. The movie is based on the life and death of General George Armstrong Custer; Errol was Custer. Think of the great performance Robert DeNiro gave in *Raging Bull*. DeNiro became Jake Lamotta right before your eyes and there was little or no doubt you were watching an award winning performance. The fact was, DeNiro did win the Academy Award, but Errol Flynn's performance is equal to that of DeNiro in many aspects. Besides getting a good review, Errol's name was never mentioned as a candidate for the Academy Award, or any award for that matter. The performance Errol gave was so touching and moving that it truly needs to be re-visited, and by all means, re-evaluated. Errol mastered the various stages in General Custer's life, beginning with his days as a cadet at West Point. The many dilemmas General Custer faced, not only in battle, but with his superiors. During the years Custer served in The Civil War, Errol Flynn's interpretation of these years was so believable the viewer felt exactly how Custer must have felt during this period of his life. The culmination of Custer's life was surely not unexpected and everyone in the theater knew he was going to die at Little Big Horn, but the way Errol Flynn prepared himself and the audience was one of the most moving scenes in all of cinema. Errol confronts his wife, played by Olivia de Havilland, on the eve of the big battle at The Little Big Horn, it is time for General Custer to say goodbye for the last time. Even though I have seen the movie numerous times, the scene the mood

Adventures of Don Juan, 1949

set by the soundtrack and the look in Errol's eyes always manages to bring me to tears. If for some reason you doubt the validity of this claim, please seek out the movie and you too will be convinced. There is one more strange fact regarding that memorable touching scene between Errol Flynn and Olivia de Havilland, ironically it was the last scene they would ever play in together and the movie was the last teaming for both. It was a truly masterful performance by Errol. The range of emotions and screen presence came across in a very natural way, Errol was Custer.

Alan Hale in *Adventures of Don Juan*

Errol Flynn as Don Juan de Marana

Don Juan ready for action

One of the largest sets of its day in *Adventures of Don Juan*

Alan Hale and Errol Flynn planning their escape

"There is a little bit of Don Juan in every man, but since I am Don Juan, there must be more of it in me!"

Barbara Stanwyck in *Cry Wolf*, 1947

Adventures of Captain Fabian, 1951

Faye Emerson in *Uncertain Glory*, 1944

The Dawn Patrol, 1938

Uncertain Glory

Castle scene in *The Warriors*, 1955

Joan Blondell in *The Perfect Specimen*, 1937

William Frawley and Alexis Smith in *Gentleman Jim*, 1942

Cast of *Gentleman Jim*

A focused Gentleman Jim

Sante Fe Trail

Lionel Atwill in *Captain Blood*

Ann Sheridan in *Silver River*, 1948

Cast of *Silver River*

The Sun Also Rises, 1957

Mel Ferrer, Errol Flynn, Ava Gardner and Eddie Albert in *The Sun Also Rises*

Paul Picerni, Raymond Burr, and Nestor Paiva in *Mara Maru*, 1952

Paul Picerni and Raymond Burr in *Mara Maru*

Ruth Roman in *Mara Maru*

Ruth Roman in *Mara Maru*

The interrogation in *Mara Maru*

Paul Picerni in *Mara Maru*

Raymond Burr and Michael Ross in *Mara Maru*

Northern Pursuit, 1943

Julie Bishop in *Northern Pursuit*

Northern Pursuit reporters

Errol in costume in *Northern Pursuit*

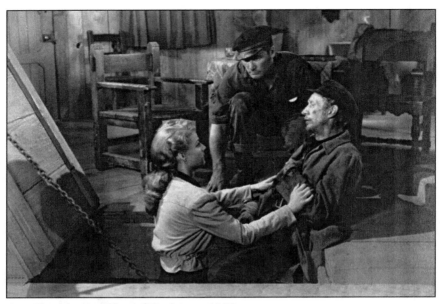

Ann Sheridan in *Edge of Darkness*, 1943

Ronald Reagan and Arthur Kennedy in *Desperate Journey*, 1942

Ronald Reagan, Alan Hale and Arthur Kennedy in *Desperate Journey*

Alan Hale, Ronald Reagan and Arthur Kennedy in *Desperate Journey*

Nancy Coleman in *Desperate Journey*

The Master of Ballantrae, 1953

A tender moment with Beatrice Campbell in *The Master of Ballantrae*

Clint Eastwood, almost ten-years after the death of Errol, starred in the Dollars Trilogy in 1967. *The Good, the Bad, and the Ugly, A Fistful of Dollars*, and *For a Few Dollars More* are considered as the definitive Westerns. The character Clint Eastwood created, the man with no name, was good and very entertaining, but lacked the range that Errol Flynn brought to all of his Western role interpretations. The main difference is that Errol could be just as mean and diabolical as Clint, but Errol could also charm the audience with his animated nature. One sly smile from Errol and a few choice words to go with the smile and it was more convincing than fifty of Clint Eastwood sneers. From an athletic standpoint, Errol was far more agile in his horseback riding skills, which included jumping on the horse, and Errol was also a better runner. One unique fact regarding Clint Eastwood's career involves Sean Connery. When Sean Connery decided to leave the James Bond franchise, Clint Eastwood was actually offered the role of James Bond. Obviously Clint turned it down. If Errol was still around at the time, he might have been one of the choices to fill the shoes of Sean Connery.

If you are keeping track of Errol Flynn's cinematic achievements so far, let's recap. *The Adventures of Robin Hood* is undoubtedly the greatest action adventure film of all time. Errol Flynn was Robin Hood in every sense of the word. *Captain Blood* and *The Sea Hawk* were the two greatest pirate movies of all time. Errol Flynn not only starred in both masterpieces, but he emulated and completely became those two pirates. *They Died with Their Boots On* has been acclaimed as the quintessential Western movie and, once again, Errol Flynn became General Custer. Errol Flynn was not only portraying each and every one of the aforementioned characters, he made you, the viewer, feel he *was* them. There would be no nominations or awards. Sadly, Errol Flynn was always overlooked.

CHAPTER 5:
Another James Bond, Indiana Jones or Dirty Harry

"I felt like an impostor, taking all that money for reciting ten or twelve lines of nonsense a day."

Errol Flynn was so natural in all of his performances a very strange concept entered my mind as I continued to bring his short, but memorable journey through his life to you the reader. It is unfortunate that out of all the Hollywood leading men who along with Errol became icons during the golden age of movies, Errol Flynn is truly the forgotten one. Certainly everyone knows about James Cagney, he will always be remembered as one of the great gangster actors, as was Edward G. Robinson. True, James Cagney was quite an actor, nominated several times for the Academy Award and even won for *Yankee Doodle Dandy*, but could it be said that Errol Flynn was just as qualified? How about the fact that Edward G. Robinson was never nominated for an Academy Award, but in 1973 the Academy decided to give him what was termed as a honorary Oscar? Spencer Tracy was also one of Hollywood's superstars during the Golden Age of cinema, and as fate would have it was nominated for nine Academy Awards, winning the best actor category on two occasions for *Captains Courageous* and *Boys Town*. The role of Father Flanagan in *Boys Town* was unique, spot on, and deserving of the Oscar. However, he was even nominated for a posthumous best actor Oscar for *Guess Who's Coming to Dinner?* Tracy didn't win this time around. Then there was Humphrey Bogart, regarded as a cultural icon, but could you always understand what he was saying? Bogey was nominated for a total of three Academy Awards and won, once for his role in *The African Queen*, yet most movie buffs feel his most famous character in *Casablanca*, Rick Blaine, should have also given him the Oscar. Turning to Henry Fonda, it was more of the same.

Henry was nominated three times for the Academy Award. Henry Fonda not only won an Academy Award for *On Golden Pond*, the Academy also decided to honor him again with a Lifetime Achievement Oscar. When you remember Gary Cooper you immediately think of a soft spoken cowboy who was nominated no less than five times and walked away with the Oscar for his roles in *Sergeant York* and *High Noon*. In 1961 the Academy also gave him an Honorary Oscar. Where in this illustrious list of fine actors is Errol Flynn? Where are the nominations set aside for Errol, in *The Adventures of Robin Hood*, Errol Flynn turned in one of the most memorable performances of any actors career, Errol was most definitely Robin Hood. The audience was treated to, not only a great action adventure movie, but Errol's performance truly rose above the scope and magnitude of the movie itself. How can the Academy ignore such a diversified body of work? Any segment of Errol's career stands alone and for arguments sake each one could be recognized. It is without question that the pirate movies Errol Flynn starred in are one of his bodies of work that relegates a renewed evaluation by the current governing board at the Academy. Errol Flynn's pirate movies were decades away from the modern pirate sagas that are enhanced by the use of special effects. The past several years one of the most successful movie franchises, *Pirates of the Caribbean*, uses special effects during almost every scene in the movie. Johnny Depp is good as Captain Jack Sparrow, but not great. The movie was created to be a commercial success and from a monetary standpoint the four chapters to date have been just that. If you ask fans of the movie franchise, I am convinced all will agree the very first movie, *Pirates of the Caribbean*, was by far the best, and the second, third and fourth versions have gone downhill respectively. There has even been a discussion recently that the third *Pirates of the Caribbean* movie was rushed to the big screen with little or no screenplay. From an acting standpoint, Captain Jack as portrayed by Johnny Depp also lost his appeal after the second movie and his performance in the third chapter is a very lackluster one. *Captain Blood* was never boring and Errol Flynn was never boring in the title role. Keep in mind it was Errol's very first shot at a major studio's signature movie production at that time. The complete performance Errol turned in can only be described as a four star one. Several years later, Errol took on another pirate role in *The Sea Hawk*, the results were exactly the same, first, *The Sea Hawk* was never boring and Errol Flynn was never boring. Errol turned in still another four star performance and it was his presence that made *The Sea Hawk* a rousing success. Even years later as Errol Flynn's career was winding down Errol made another pirate move, *Against All Flags*. At the time, the movie was shot Errol was going on forty-four years of age and he still managed to upstage a much younger Anthony Quinn. If you need some additional proof of just how much Errol always wanted to get the most out of all his performances, he actually broke an ankle near the end of the production. Errol was also quite ill during much of the filming, but unless you look closely and had not been made aware of this fact, you would have never known how sick he really was. In the following year, Errol once again picked up his sword and began production on another action adventure movie that you could say is in the same category as his pirate movies, *The Master of Ballantrae*. The additional year Errol had added to his age actually did wonders for him and by all accounts he looked and moved like a twenty year old once again. Errol was trying to regain his popularity by making movies in Europe. *The Master of Ballantrae* was shot entirely in England and Scotland and was a success in the United States. The very next year, 1954, Errol Flynn made another action adventure movie, this time in Italy. The name of this production was *Crossed Swords* and Errol's leading lady was one of the most popular Italian actresses at the time, Gina Lollobrigida. The movie should be discussed, because the character that Errol portrayed in this movie was not unlike Captain Jack Sparrow. The comparison has to be made, because Errol makes sure from the very first scene in the movie the audience knows he is playing out the role 100% tongue-in-cheek. It can also be said that the character, Renzo, that Errol portrays, has a lot more charm than Captain Jack Sparrow. It was not a successful movie in the States because the production company, United Artists, failed to promote it.

In 1954, Errol had truly had enough of all the Hollywood politics. Errol knew all too well that he had been used and really taken advantage of. It was part of what Hollywood was really all about, when you are young and famous, you are young and famous. When you are old and famous in Hollywood, you are just old. While filming the movie *Crossed Swords* in Italy, Errol decided to form his own production company and bring to the screen the well-known story of William Tell. It was an epic adventure and one of the first to be shot in CinemaScope at a cost of over $860,000. To date there was only one movie that was shot in the new CinemaScope process, *The Robe* and it had not been released. It was by all accounts going to be a rousing success and a big financial boom for Errol who was investing everything he had to the production. The countryside of Italy was a perfect locale and a village was being constructed to add to the authenticity of the movie. Errol had even cleaned up his act and was perhaps the best shape he had been in a least a decade. The co-stars and hundreds of extras were eager to get the movie off the ground. When Errol tested several young Italian actresses for leading roles, one in particular he didn't like and rejected her screen test; the girl was Sophia Loren. The first several days of shooting went very smooth and Errol was in very high spirits. Unfortunately, the Italian backers who were going to fund the project backed out soon after the start of the third week and Errol's dream of *The Story of William Tell* was shattered. This ill-fated venture would prove to be too much for Errol to bear and he was literally a broken man. Faced with the prospect of multiple lawsuits, Errol was literally broke for the first time in his life. Errol also found out that the Internal Revenue Service back in the states was after hundreds of thousands of back taxes. This important piece of the Errol Flynn legacy was mentioned, because all of the other stars of this era were good, but only Errol Flynn was so dedicated that in order to prove himself one more time as a great actor, he took it upon himself to attempt a blockbuster movie on his own. It might have been the role that finally woke up Hollywood and forced them to recognized Errol as the great actor he truly was.

"Bond, James Bond"—stop and think of Errol Flynn uttering those famous words. When you hear those words for the first time it conjures up thoughts of the suave sophisticated super spy. Perhaps you should try and obtain a few of the Errol Flynn movies where Errol didn't wear a cowboy hat, ride a horse of weld a sword. Errol just might impress you one more time with his undaunted ability to play any role. However, before the comparison of Errol Flynn to the numerous actors who played James Bond is made, let's take a look at some additional facts relative to the quest for recognition,

Errol on his yacht

Time doesn't stand still—check the clock

well deserved recognition. Two of the most prestigious universities that specialized in movie related curriculums, New York University, in lower Manhattan, and USC in Southern California, seldom, if ever refer to the works of Errol Flynn. These universities, as well as, hundreds of universities across the United States have omitted Errol completely. It is unfortunate that the generations that followed Errol didn't have more exposure to his unique approach to acting and the many different characters he created. I trust that as you read this special account of Errol's influence in the movie industry you will be curious enough and motivated to experience some of the movies described so far. It has been said that you can lead a horse to water, but can you make him drink. If you take the advice of the author and watch the movies, then draw your own conclusions, I am convinced it will be the beginning of many new and exciting movie adventures you never knew existed. It will be evident that the casual, natural acting style that Errol conveyed, coupled with his unique persona, and striking good looks were so unique that Errol will be able to build on his forgotten legacy, even today. Most, if not all of the actors during the days when Errol was in Hollywood, seem slightly frozen in time. They wouldn't fit in today's movies, would they? They didn't have today's look. Errol was different; he stood out, and I think I have touched on one of the main reasons why, Errol was contemporary, and always had a contemporary look. You can take a scene from one of Errol's movies, and you can literally put that scene in a 2011 film and he most definitely would look like he belongs. For example, Errol worked with some of the greatest directors of the era, of course these same directors worked with other actors, but if you compare movies that have Errol as the star to comparative movies made at the same time in Hollywood, it is evident Errol always brought out the best these directors had to offer. It is time for you to evaluate the comparisons that have been described. You will see for yourself that only the movies starring Errol will appeal to you. A really good choice would be to select one of the movies that Errol made that didn't fall into the action adventure genre. Quite possibly *Gentlemen Jim*, made in 1942, is a great movie to analyze. His contemporary look in this feature and his ability to fit into the current movies will be quite evident. If you want addition material to analyze, his performance in the 1957 movie, *The Sun Also Rises*,

Errol loved his boats

lets you have a look at the aging Errol, but he still had the unique screen presence that stole each and every scene from the other actors in the movie. He was old, but still more contemporary than one of his co-stars in *The Sun Also Rises*, the great Tyrone Power, or even Eddie Albert who was also in the movie. The three actors played old friends reunited in Spain, but it was Errol who stood out and you might have a hard time convincing yourself that these three friends were from the same era at one time in their lives.

Errol on his yacht, *Zaca*

On the *Zaca* with Robin Hood's bow

Climbing the mast of *Sirocco*

Errol on the deck of *Zaca*

Vintage auto with a vintage Errol

Rare shot of Errol riding in the countryside

One evening, I decided to put the pen down for a while and watch one of Errol's movies. I was inspiring myself. Having seen every movie Errol has starred in numerous times, it would be difficult for me to make a choice. For some crazy reason, I decided to play the old eeny, meeny, miny, moe game, and strange as it may seem, I landed on one of Errol's rather obscure movies, *Cry Wolf*. It was made in 1947, and in this Warner Bros. production, Errol has a brand new leading lady, Barbara Stanwyck, and Richard Basehart as a co-star. Hollywood was obsessed during this time period with the film noir genre of movies. Most experts on the subject might argue that *Cry Wolf* is not a *film noir* movie, but it contains all of the elements that make up *film noir*. It is said that *film noir* is not a genre of films, but can be described in the following way. *Film noir* is the mood, the style, a point of view, the tone of a film. It is also helpful to note that *film noir* usually refers to a distinct historical period of film history, the decade of film making after World War II. *Film noir* is similar to the German Expressionism period or to the New Wave films of France. In the United States, the studios were making

Westerns and musicals, but never really knew that years later their dark gangster movies would be labeled as *film noir*. These movies usually contained most of the same elements, heroes, anti-heroes, corrupt characters, down and out villains, hard boiled detectives, corrupt cops, government agents, spies, gangsters, lone wolfs and even socio-paths, killers, politicians or just plain Joe's. Is it possible Errol Flynn actually starred in a *film noir* movie? *Cry Wolf* is so campy and has so many characters and storylines, one has to argue that it is *film noir*. Barbara Stanwyck, who was one of Warner Bros.' best leading ladies of the time, was a unique choice to be Errol's co-star. Everyone felt that there would be little or no chemistry between Errol and Barbara, but of course they were dead wrong. The result of the pairing once again proved just how good an actor Errol was, because it can be said the script was rather weak, but Errol saved the day as a "bad" guy. Errol didn't get good reviews for his performance, but I guess they didn't understand his character portrayal or were too used to the good guy hero type he was always cast in. *Cry Wolf* made me wonder and brought to mind several scenes in some James Bond movies. Certainly Errol would have been the perfect James Bond. Can anyone question that Errol had much more charm than Sean Connery? What about savoir fair, Sean Connery or Errol Flynn? If you need more proof, who looks better dressed up in a tuxedo? Who can run down a bad guy or who most definitely is the better fighter, swordsman or acrobat? The most important quality James Bond always had was of course, his way with the opposite sex. Errol Flynn was by far the master of melting hearts and charming female spies would have been as easy for Errol as ordering champagne. Once again, try to imagine Errol Flynn making his appearance for the first time and uttering those famous words, Bond, James Bond. It will be evident Errol had it all over Sean Connery. Now we have the screen test for the James Bond character, both Sean Connery and Errol Flynn have to utter the "Bond, James Bond" phrase. Errol would have received the part based solely on that screen test. Roger Moore and Pierce Brosnan were much more athletic and mobile then Sean Connery, but neither of these two actors was a match for the athletic prowess that Errol Flynn possessed. The current James Bond, Daniel Craig, possesses none of the suave characteristics Errol Flynn would have brought to the James Bond character, and once again, how can you compare Daniel Craig to Errol Flynn when it came down to charming the girls. The one element that has always been a major part of all the James Bond movies is females and what better actor could there be than Errol to melt their hearts? To be completely fair in the assessment of the James Bond evaluation relative to the prospect of Errol Flynn being cast in the role. There was one James Bond actor that was close to Errol in his look, demeanor and even his voice. That actor was probably the least favorite of all the James Bond's to date, Timothy Dalton. It would be extra special if a commercial is made with Errol cast as a James Bond type. With today's computer technology, it would be fairly easy to accomplish and prove to be very interesting.

While we are on the subject of Errol Flynn being cast in the role of a modern day hero such as James Bond, how about Indiana Jones? Perhaps it is not as far-fetched a concept as you might think. The one accolade that Errol Flynn has always received is that Errol is always considered as the greatest swashbuckling hero of all time. That label was given most likely for the roles that Errol portrayed in the pirate sagas and other period sword welding heroes. There are two of Errol's movies that have characters that one may be able to draw comparisons to the Indiana Jones character. The first is Robin Hood. Errol was constantly faced with overwhelming odds and trapped in many tight locations. In the second movie, on the surface it may not seem that this feature has any qualities where comparisons can be made to Indiana Jones. However, *The Adventures of Don Juan* finds our hero Errol at the very onset of the movie being chased off a balcony and he invites the danger with a very jovial nature. Throughout the movie, Errol was continually being chased and pursued by overwhelming odds, but each and every time he faced the danger with a smile, and most times he was laughing his way through the action. The character of Don Juan was a rather ruthless character, but at the same time, a very likeable one, and a character that was also invulnerable. Indiana Jones was created with most of those qualities, but could Harrison Ford, as Indiana Jones, leap from balconies and onto horses with the same style and grace as Errol Flynn? In some scenes, Harrison Ford lumbered through the action, in comparison with how Errol gracefully met physical challenges. Another Errol Flynn movie that comes to mind is *The Dawn Patrol*. It was a period war drama that once again showcased another masterful performance by Errol. The key elements that compare the action to an Indiana Jones movie would be the way Errol interacted with his German adversaries, as well as, his comrades. The period flight clothes that were used in *The Dawn Patrol* are also good indications that Errol looked the Indiana Jones part and the evidence is just how good these uniforms looked on him.

In one long forgotten Errol Flynn movie, Errol plays a Canadian Mounted Policeman. By a slight comparison is it possible he could have taken on the role of Dirty Harry? It was another great cowboy movie that really reminds me of *Dirty Harry* even though the time period is very far removed. It is Errol in the classic Western, *Virginia City*. This movie was released in 1940 and Errol was pitted against two of Hollywood's biggest stars at the time. Here you had the great Humphrey Bogart and the formidable Randolph Scott sharing the big screen with Errol. These heavyweight actors were no match for Errol and he literally stole the show, especially when on-screen confrontations arose. As a change of pace the studio decided that in *Virginia City* they would cast Errol in a very hard-nosed role. He was tough as nails and the personality of his character that he brings to the screen is very similar to that of the Dirty Harry one.

The epic adventure movies of the 1950s also centered on ancient Rome and Greece. It is strange that when *Quo Vadis, The Robe* or even *Demetrius and The Gladiators* were being cast Errol Flynn's name never came up. Errol had made numerous period movies such as *The Private Lives of Elizabeth and Essex* and *The Prince and the Pauper*. Both of these movies were not related to Rome or Greece, but were period movies that featured lavish costumes. Errol was the one actor who always looked like the costume he wore was one that he was born to wear. Think of Errol Flynn in the role of Maximus in *The Gladiator*. Russell Crowe was pretty spectacular several years ago in *The Gladiator*, but could Errol have done a much better job in attacking the role? There was a majestic air about Maximus as he became a gladiator. He made you believe in his character and he even made the viewer pity Maximus. Errol Flynn was placed in that position in many of his roles and it would be foolish to think that Errol Flynn could not portray Maximus with more regality and feeling than Russell Crowe. It would have been one more memorable performance that would hold up today and solidify Errol's legacy as one of the greatest actors of all time. How about *Spartacus*? Surely Kirk Douglas was never nominated for the Academy Award in the title role, but perhaps if Errol was around and a few years younger when the movie was released in 1960, Errol might have received a nomination. Errol always managed to put a little extra into all of his roles, with a glance, his special smile and his dynamic sneer, they could have been just what the critics felt was missing from Spartacus.

The only way to really make sense of these speculative comparisons is to watch Errol Flynn in all of his movies. You will become completely drawn to Errol's unique style, his persona, and the Flynn-like characterizations that only Errol Flynn brought to his roles. Most definitely, you will want to see all of his movies because you will be convinced each and every one must be special, very special. Errol was the quintessential leading man.

CHAPTER 6:
Searching for the Academy Award

"It isn't what they say about you, it's what they whisper."

When you think of a career of twenty-five years in the movie industry it really seems like a very short time, but Errol Flynn's entire career in Hollywood was just that, a mere twenty-five years. Considering the fact that Errol Flynn died at the ripe old age of fifty, half of his entire life was spent as a movie actor. It is quite unusual for any actor to star in over fifty films, but even though Errol was only an actor for about twenty five or so years, he is credited with being in sixty-two movies. In those movies, he began as a corpse and ended up somewhere in Cuba as a freedom fighter, a man of adventure. When you watch Errol in the many roles he brought to the screen, the one basic trait Errol had was complete control of each and every character he portrayed. In the two most famous pirate movies Errol starred in, *Captain Blood* and *The Sea Hawk*, the two pirates he portrayed were completely different. In the first movie, *Captain Blood*, Errol is Captain Peter Blood, a physician condemned to slavery after being caught treating a rebel. Even though the production values of the movie are far superior of any current pirate saga, it is clearly Errol and the mood he brings forth in the role that make *Captain Blood* one of the greatest swashbuckling movies of all time. If you have never had the pleasure of seeing it first hand, you must seek it out and you will be more than impressed. When Warner Bros. was looking for still another vehicle for their superstar Errol to rake in revenue, they settled on *The Sea Hawk*. Once again Errol is a pirate, but unlike his role in *Captain Blood* this time around he has matured from the boyish pirate to the commanding leader of a scurry bunch of cutthroats. Some critics feel Errol was at his peak in this adaptation, but I say Errol was always at his peak and his interpretation of Geoffrey Thorpe is flawless. Errol played pirates in several other movies but these are the two definitive pirate sagas that you must seek out, I guarantee you will watch them more than once. *Captain Blood* received a nomination for the best picture, but even though it was Errol Flynn who made the movie a success he was never nominated and Victor McLaglen won for his role in *The Informer*. In 1940, the year *The Sea Hawk* was released, James Stewart walked home with the Oscar for his role in *The Philadelphia Story*. These two actors were seasoned veterans in the movie business and when Errol made *Captain Blood* he was a raw talent, who not only won the hearts of every woman in the world, but every guy wanted to be like him. As was previously stated, the performance was an earnest and gallant performance that coupled with his raw talent should have at the least been nominated. The so called experts probably felt it was just one of those hap-instances but they were all shocked a few years later when Errol did it again, and again, and again.

Errol managed to turn in two very unique and memorable performances in the years following *Captain Blood*, three years to be exact. The critics were not very impressed with the performance Errol gave in *They Died With Their Boots On*, even though Errol managed to upstage each and every seasoned male actor in the cast. The movie was a box office sensation and Errol's legions of fans were growing faster than any other star in the early 1940s both male and female. The bosses at Warner Bros. were well aware of the growing popularity of their young leading man and of course wanted to crank out as many movies that they could with Errol's name at top billing. If the critics were not willing to recognize Errol's role as Custer in the *They Died with their Boots On* saga, surely they had to recognize Errol's total performance in *The Adventures of Robin Hood*. The year was 1938 and Hollywood had its share of really great actors, for instance many seasoned veterans such as Basil Rathbone, Claude Rains and Patric Knowles shared the screen with Errol in Robin Hood, but it was clearly Errol who made each and every scene memorable. It didn't matter that the movie, *The Adventures of Robin Hood*, made millions for the studio, and helped a sagging box office in America bounce back. It didn't matter that most critics were in agreement finally that Errol Flynn was a force to reckon with in

Hollywood. It also didn't matter that most movie goers decided that this was a movie so entertaining that they went to see it again and again. Keep in mind the movie fan of 1939 had no DVD player to use when they wanted to see a favorite movie again; they had to buy another ticket. With all these factors in place, sadly *The Adventures of Robin Hood* and Errol Flynn the star never received a nomination. The best picture for the year 1939 was *You Can't Take it with You*, and Spencer Tracy won the best actor award for his performance in *Boy's Town*, his second best actor award in a row. If you evaluate the leading men in the case of Spencer Tracy vs. Errol Flynn, and the movies, *Robin Hood* vs. *Boys Town*, it will be a very good exercise and will hopefully convince you that not only was Errol Flynn deserving of a nomination for his performance in *The Adventures of Robin Hood*, but that the production of the movie was definitely deserving of the nomination it received. Unfortunately, it didn't win.

If anyone wanted to critique Errol's versatility, if anyone wanted to evaluate his acting ability, and if anyone wanted to question the argument relative to Errol being recognized by the Academy, let's look at several other great performances turned in by Errol. Following on the heels of the box office smash hit, *They Died with their Boots On*, Warner Brother cast Errol in the role of one of the most charismatic boxers ever to enter the ring. *Gentleman Jim* was the biography of James J. Corbett, and if an actor could capture all the different qualities Corbett's personality had, surely Errol would give it his best shot. The movie was filled with some of the biggest Hollywood established actors of the day, names that everyone remembers from the 1940s, among them Alan Hale, who played James Corbett's father, a favorite co-star of Errol's who also became one of Errol's life-long friends. How about William Frawley, who will always be remembered as Lucy and Desi's friend and landlord, Fred Mertz? Then there was the outstanding character actor, Jack Carson, and John Loder a veteran actor who had over 110 movie credits to his name. If you needed one more male actor to round out this cast of distinguished actors, James Corbett's rival in the movie was John L. Sullivan, and enter Ward Bond who played Sullivan to a tea. The movie was not without female stars and one of the most beautiful and talented actresses of her day, Alexis Smith, was cast in the role of Errol's love interest, a role she would reprise with Errol in the

Alexis Smith as Jeanne Starr in *San Antonio*

Western saga *San Antonio*. When you watch this movie for the first time and about half way through the production, it will be evident that Errol Flynn is probably, no make that most definitely, the only actor to ever grace the silver screen that can be arrogant, obnoxious, and still have you like him. *Gentleman Jim* the movie, by all accounts, is one of the best sports movies of all time. It is unfortunate that *Gentleman Jim* is not even listed in the greatest boxing movie category and also omitted from the greatest sports movie list. The aforementioned leading men and lady are overshadowed by the performance Errol Flynn gave. The arrogance, the charm, the bold approach to the role should have rendered Errol Flynn numerous accolades, but Hollywood refused to recognize Errol, even though he continued to grow as an actor and continued to make large sums of revenue for the studios. This performance cannot be overlooked and should be on the list of re-visited movies that Errol Flynn starred in when the Academy decides that Errol most certainly deserves a second look as a candidate for a posthumous award. One very unique characteristic that Errol Flynn had in *Gentleman Jim* was how right from the beginning of the movie, Errol was a very abrasive man, or

Errol Flynn as Clay Hardin in *San Antonio*, 1945

should I say James J. Corbett was, not only a rogue, but someone that most movie goers disliked immediately. Here is where only Errol Flynn could, by perhaps twenty or thirty minutes later, turn those same viewers around one hundred percent, they loved James J. Corbett, they loved Errol Flynn. It is an overlooked quality that you will never find in any other actor's performances. Errol Flynn was one of a kind, and when you entertain, bring in large sums of revenue to the studios that you work for, your industry should recognize you.

Alexis Smith in *San Antonio*

Bar scene in *San Antonio*

Street scene in *San Antonio*

Jeanne and Clay heading for San Antonio in a stage coach

Guinn (Big Boy) Williams and Alan Hale in *Virginia City*, 1940

Antonella Lualdi in *William Tell*, unfinished

William Tell

On the set of *William Tell*

William Tell on set in Italy

In this early age of Hollywood, the country was faced with wars, depression and the overall tone of morality; they frowned upon the behavior that Errol Flynn displayed when the cameras were turned off. It was not easy for a man like Errol Flynn to separate himself from the roles he was cast in. Errol Flynn was James J. Corbett, a wild and crazy guy, long before that term was widely used. Errol Flynn most definitely was the embodiment of Sir Robin of Locksley, Robin Hood, when he welcomed Lady Marian and Sir Guy to Sherwood forest. It was evident that Errol really had a personality which contained all of Robin Hood's qualities. When you delve deeper into his performances each and every one is unique, but they all have an underpinning of mischief. The studios and perhaps the Academy which viewed Errol Flynn's off-screen antics, unfortunately took it upon themselves to stop any and all attempts to recognized Errol Flynn's dynamic performances, because of his behavior. They should have overlooked Errol Flynn's outlandish behavior and recognized Errol for his contribution to the movie industry. The movie industry is driven by box office results and most definitely all of Errol Flynn's movies were solid performers in that category. The movie industry should have looked at how quickly Errol Flynn's performances attracted the movie industries' most important commodity, the movie-going public. Errol Flynn had legions of fans almost immediately when they first caught a glimpse of Errol on the big screen. It was impossible not to be taken in by his approach to playing roles, it was impossible not to like him, or in the case of the female fans, not to fall in love with Errol Flynn.

The most influential man in Hollywood during the time period of Errol Flynn's greatest success was, Jack L. Warner, and as fate would have it he just happened to be Errol's boss so to speak. Jack L. Warner was the head of Warner Bros. Studios and it was no secret that Errol Flynn and Mr. Warner had an ongoing feud that lasted throughout Errol's motion picture contract with Warner Bros. Pictures. When the nominations for the Academy Awards were decided each and every year during the time when Errol Flynn was at his peak, the probability of Jack L. Warner having a big influence in the choices is quite high. Add to that factor, the many influential business, and non-business associates, Jack Warner had, and it adds up to one of the reasons Errol Flynn was never even nominated for the prestigious Academy Award. Rumors were widely circulating that Errol Flynn was carrying on with several Hollywood studio heads wives. It was no secret that Errol was the most sought after male actor by all women, and perhaps of all time. There were other actors who also had reputations of being ladies men, but none could ever come close to the escapades of Errol Flynn. Getting back to Errol's relationship with the Warner Bros. Studio and Jack L. Warner; here we have the brazenness of

Errol Flynn taking off in the middle of a multi-million dollar movie production, where he is the main attraction. Well, it wasn't that Errol Flynn somehow decided he needed a sick day, he decided he need a full vacation. Errol Flynn loved adventure, he loved sailing the seven seas, and visiting tropical islands, so that is exactly what Errol Flynn did. Right smack dab in the middle of one of Warner Bros.' feature films Errol Flynn got on his boat and took off to some unknown destination. As far as having any concern for what his adventure would mean to the movie production he was the major star of, Errol showed little or in fact no concern. It was an era when there were no cell phones, no internet and once you left the mainland wherever the movie was being produced, in all effect you were missing in action. Errol Flynn loved to take off a week or two from making a movie and sail the seas in one of his ships, in this case *The Zaca*. It can be noted that even today Errol Flynn's favorite port, Port Antonio in Jamaica, has a full-service marina that bears his name. In defense of the way Errol Flynn conducted himself during these mysterious adventures, Errol Flynn was never giving the respect he so rightfully deserved by the Studios. It must have been very difficult to realize the amount of money Errol Flynn generated on a regular basis in his mind. It must have been very difficult for Errol Flynn to read all the accolades that the press showed relative to how successful an actor he was from a dollars and cents evaluation. Here was the studios biggest asset and Errol Flynn knew he was not respected for his talent. Errol Flynn realized in many ways he was being used. Keep in mind Errol Flynn was a multi-faceted individual. Errol Flynn was the most handsome actor of all time, the original swashbuckler, and more importantly, Errol Flynn was highly intellectual. The apple doesn't fall far from the tree, as the saying goes, Errol Flynn was the son of a professor and a visionary.

When Errol was travelling around the globe, long before Errol Flynn knew that Hollywood or perhaps even the motion picture movie industry existed, he contracted malaria, a dreadful disease that never left his body and when he had a re-occurring bout with malaria he was sometimes unable to act or even show up on the set. Now we have Jack L. Warner funding a production and his star is causing multiple delays in production. It most definitely was a factor in the movie industry and the Academy's decision to omit Errol Flynn from the Oscar nominees.

In all fairness to the many influential detractors in Hollywood who will look at this evaluation of Errol Flynn and the many reasons why he never received an Academy Award nomination a comparison of other actors follows. Many great actors during the era of Errol Flynn's motion picture performances truly deserved the Academy Awards they won in the best actor category. Some, like Sir Lawrence Olivier, one of Hollywood's greatest actors of all time, once referred to Errol Flynn as an actor that he would have liked to work with. Humphrey Bogart who did work with Errol Flynn had the greatest respect for Errol and in the one movie that they made together, Errol actually stole all the scenes from Bogart. Keep in mind, Bogart is one of those iconic actors that is revered for decades after his death and some of his films are true Hollywood classics. Gary Cooper was an Academy Award winner and one could argue if he was truly a greater actor than Errol Flynn, it really does lend itself to controversy for sure. One last great actor who was at his peak during his Godfather years, but did have some roles during the same time as some of Errol Flynn's movies was Marlon Brando. In the mid-fifties, Brando burst onto the scene with his Stanislavski System of acting he picked up in the New School's dramatic section. Marlon Brando also attended numerous other acting classes. While in comparison, Errol Flynn had no formal training. Most, if not all of Marlon Brando's early roles, such as *A Streetcar Named Desire, On the Waterfront* and *The Wild One,* all established Marlon Brando as one of top Hollywood actors of the fifties. These movies had characters that Marlon Brando portrayed in his "method acting" technique. He also used this technique in his portrayal of Mark Anthony in *Julius Caesar.* Imagine a young Errol Flynn cast in these roles and how he would have approached each one. If you think about how spot-on Errol always was with his performances, the many varied roles Errol had, it might be still another comparison that can and should shed new light on the quest to have Errol Flynn recognized by the industry that he gave so much to.

There was one final attempt at an aging Errol Flynn to once again show the movie-going public and his critics that he really was a great actor, one deserving of so much more than ridicule and tabloid fodder. In 1957, who knew that in a short two years Errol Flynn would be dead, his once bright shining star gone forever? But 1957 held a wonderful chapter in the all too short life of Errol Flynn.

Sometimes referred to as the greatest modernist novel ever written was being brought to the big screen. It was Ernest Hemingway's *The Sun Also Rises*. The novel was based on Hemingway's own trip to Spain in 1925. The plot is about a group of old friends who travel from Paris to the Festival of San Fermin, in Pamplona, Spain, for the yearly running of the bulls. The novel setting was considered unique and memorable, presenting the seedy café life of Paris and the Pamplona festival. When the studio, 20th Century-Fox, invested over five million dollars on a movie they wanted it to make money. In order to guarantee a successful return at the box office the cast had to have big marquee names. Keep in mind the characters in Ernest Hemingway's novel were up in age so the studio needed big stars who were also near the end of their careers. It would be a big gamble because in the late 1950s the movie going public was a fickle one and wanted fresh and new actors and actresses in the movies they paid to view. Top billing in *The Sun Also Rises* went to Tyrone Power, a matinee idol who had not aged gracefully and he was exactly who the studio needed to play the American news correspondent Jake Barnes, who, after incurring a injury in WWI that has rendered him impotent, relocates to Paris to escape his troubles. Barnes links up with several other lost souls, including the nymphomaniacal Lady Brett Ashley, so aptly cast by one of the most beautiful actresses of her day, Ava Gardner. The reason why so much detail is being made regarding the movie and the cast is to allow the reader to evaluate the performances of these great actors and actresses relative to the performance Errol Flynn delivered. Some of the more notable actors were the close friends of Tyrone Powers character Jake Barnes, they were perennial hangers-on in the movie, Robert Cohn played by Mel Ferrer, and Bill Gorton played by Eddie Albert. In their never-ending search for new thrills, Barnes and his cohorts trundle off to Spain, where they participate in the annual Pamplona bull run and act as unofficial "sponsors" of handsome young matador Pedro Romero (played by future film executive Robert Evans). A recent movie, *The Kid Stays in the Picture*, is a semi-documentary revolving around Robert Evans and how they wanted him removed from the production. The last and most dynamic character was Mike Campbell, played by Errol Flynn. Mike was a very hedonistic, hard-drinking, and truly burnt-out soul. Even though the critics argued that it was Errol Flynn merely playing himself, it was just a realization of who and what the once great star was, they couldn't put aside the great performance Errol Flynn gave. The performance Errol Flynn turned in was the one that truly carried the entire production.

It has to be noted that somewhere in the media during the time leading up to the Academy Award nominations, Errol Flynn's performance was mentioned as being nominated for his performance in *The Sun Also Rises*. When word of the nomination reached Errol he was extremely surprised because deep down inside he was aware of the reputation that followed him throughout his illustrious career. As fate would have it, the nomination strangely vanished and it was never mentioned again until recently in an Australian Documentary about the life of Errol Flynn. It can also be noted that Errol was extremely happy and proud that finally, after all these years, he was being recognized. In an ironic twist of fate the nomination for his performance in *The Sun Also Rises* sadly turned out to be just a rumor. Errol carried the burden of never being nominated for any of his performances for decades and, even now, at the dawn of his life, he was disappointed one more time. Hopefully after reading this book, and seeking out the body of work that Errol Flynn was responsible for you, the reader will be impressed enough and moved to the point where you agree that a posthumous recognition award from the Academy is justified and long overdue.

Cary Grant was a great actor, he had a remarkable charm and he was always, like Errol Flynn, a major box office draw. Cary Grant was nominated for an Oscar on two occasions for best actor. Once in 1941 for his role in *Penny Serenade* and then again in 1944 for his performance in *None But The Lonely Heart*. Even though he lost in both of those nominations, in 1970 Cary Grant was presented with an honorary Oscar and the statement read "for his unique mastery of the art of screen acting with the respect and affection of his colleagues." Cary Grant was also nominated for no less than five

Golden Globes, he lost all five times. That is a total of seven best actor nominations and not a single win, but the Academy wanted to recognize his acting ability in any case.

Errol Flynn was the Hollywood bad boy of that era, his reputation as a womanizer was legendary. Errol Flynn was married three times. It can be noted that Cary Grant was a favorite of the studios and looked upon in a much different light than Errol Flynn; however, Mr. Grant was married five times. That alone by the sheer number of marriages that Cary Grant entered in would also categorize Mr. Grant as a womanizer. Getting back to the Oscar nominations that Cary Grant received, first in 1941 for *Penny Serenade* a movie that really didn't move the critics, but because of the subject matter, a husband and wife adopting a baby after their own child dies suddenly, it was well received by the movie-going public. In reviews, it has been noted that several of the supporting actors actually were better than Cary Grant. The movie was basically a very sentimental tearjerker and in many ways the reason for Cary Grant's nomination. Errol Flynn was starring in a big movie in the year 1941, *They Died With Their Boots On*. The performance Errol Flynn turned in as General Custer and the movie itself are heads above the afore-mentioned *Penny Serenade*. It was just one more indication of how sometimes no matter how good an actor you are, if your reputation precedes you, it will be impossible to get the recognition you aptly deserve.

Moving ahead to the comparison of Cary Grant to Errol Flynn, in 1944, Cary Grant once again was nominated for an Oscar, this time in a dramatic role in *None But The Lonely Heart*. Is that performance much better than Errol Flynn's performance in the 1944 movie *Uncertain Glory*? At best, the two performances are equal and if you consider that Errol Flynn was the biggest action adventure hero of that era, he was cast in a dramatic role that Errol Flynn was extremely good at.

This is just one more documented comparison of the unique acting skills that Errol Flynn possessed and was always overlooked.

During the last fifty or so years after Errol Flynn died at the age of fifty in 1959, many other actors have received Academy Awards, not for a specific role in a movie, but for their body of work. It is time for Flynn to finally be recognized for not only what has been described in this book, but for his unique and lasting impressions. *Errol Flynn: the Quest for an Oscar* is even more appropriate after these comparisons.

CHAPTER 7:
From Pitcairn Island to Cuba

"If I have any genius it is a genius for living."

The exciting voyage of Errol Flynn began in the majestic beauty of Pitcairn Island and ended up some twenty-six years later in a seedy barren jungle in Cuba. Errol Flynn was in his early twenties when he was on Pitcairn Island and fifty-years-old in that Cuban jungle. It was, however, a voyage of Errol Flynn that the public got to follow in many ways on the big screen. It can be said that sandwiched in between those short twenty-six years are some of the greatest performances ever to grace the silver screen. Those very memorable, artistic interpretations surely deserve a much closer evaluation. Errol Flynn was a pirate, a doctor, a cowboy, a knight in shining armor, a pilot in the Air Force, a soldier in the army infantry, a spy, a championship boxer and a seeker of fortune. Errol Flynn was royalty, a writer, a Canadian Mounted policeman, a criminal, a composer, a financier and a skin diver. Then Errol Flynn was a Prince, a croupier, a British Army officer, a General, an alcoholic, a research scientist, a commercial artist, a husband and father, an aristocrat, a horse trader in India, an aging film star and a king. Finally, Errol Flynn was an adventurer in those jungles of Cuba, but of course he also played the role he was destined for in *The Adventures of Don Juan*.

All of the many characters Errol Flynn played on the big screen were a testimony to his unique range and complete acting ability. One seemingly overlooked quality that Errol Flynn possessed was Errol's gift of how Errol looked in costume. This characteristic was another that truly set Errol Flynn apart from his peers. The moment Errol Flynn donned a costume he appeared as if he was made to wear it all his life. It instantly made you believe that Errol Flynn was an officer in *The Charge of the Light Brigade*. Real aristocrats of knights never even came close to the ones that Errol Flynn portrayed, because you might say it was Errol's looks and demeanor that brought out what a uniform is meant to convey. Then there were the impeccable vocal ranges and facial overtones that only Errol Flynn had in overabundance. It would be almost impossible to make comparisons regarding Errol Flynn's ability to "wear it well" in regard to costume melodramas he was cast in to other actors' portrayals. Likewise, it would be most difficult to select a performance relative to the costume, or uniform's distinctive quality of Errol Flynn in uniform because all of those performances stand out. The depictions stand out mainly because Errol Flynn always made sure of that in his casual believable approach.

The following is a collection of the roles that have become favorites, even of the critics, most of whom never embraced Errol Flynn. It can also be said that most, if not all, of the great actors of Errol Flynn's era always needed some fabricated gossip to generate interest for their fans. Errol however on the other hand delivered all the controversy and scandal that his fans knew would eclipse the other non-interesting rival actors.

It is time to take a much closer look at some of Errol Flynn's most memorable performances. *Gentlemen Jim*, was Errol Flynn's 20th Hollywood release, and he was cast in the role of James J. Corbett, the heavyweight boxer who defeated the great John L. Sullivan. Errol was not only believable during all the scenes as Corbett in ring boxing, but his endearing performance ran the gamut of emotions. This film proved once again how Errol Flynn could hold the audience in the palm of his hand and his on screen chemistry with his female co-star, Alexis Smith was right on. When the scenes called for Errol to act opposite his male co-star Ward Bond, as John L. Sullivan, Errol can only be compared to the great superstars of his day. The warmth and camaraderie Errol displayed to John L. was truly a work of art. One scene in particular, when Errol beats John L. for the heavyweight title, is perhaps one of the most touching scenes between two prize fighters who just had a monumental bout in motion picture history. When John L. Sullivan hands Errol Flynn the championship belt, instead of a sense of shear victory, the emotional look, feel that Errol conveys in the touching scene truly brought the audience to tears.

The first few years of the 1940s saw Hollywood cranking out pirate movies. Some of the rival studios produced such blockbuster hits as, *The Black Swan* with Tyrone Power in the lead role. *The Spanish Main* starring Paul Henreid and *Frenchman's Creek* with Basil Rathbone, all lit up the screen with high adventure. These action adventure movies brought in the most revenue during that time period but the one quality they all lacked was a bone fide cult hero. Warner Bros., Errol Flynn's employer in the 1940s decided to throw their hat in the ring and decided to try their luck one more time mainly because of the outstanding success they had with Errol Flynn's first blockbuster, the 1935, *Captain Blood.* The studio and Jack Warner in particular wanted to take no chances and he personally ran the project. Mr. Warner decided to surround his new star with many seasoned veterans, and he assembled a stellar cast led by Claude Rains, Donald Crisp, Alan Hale and Brenda Marshall. Jack Warner was a gambler, but he knew it would be near impossible to make a better pirate epic than the highly successful *Captain Blood*, but he rolled the dice and came up with another winner. It was the remarkable performance that Errol Flynn turned in that not only proved to Jack Warner and the studio he ran, they had the golden boy, Errol struck gold again. The movie was based on a novel by Rafael Sabatini, *The Sea Hawk* and remains, even to this day, as perhaps the greatest pirate adventure movies of all time. It was Errol Flynn who electrified the screen albeit without any special effects, Errol was all the special effects the movie needed. The one drawback of this epic adventure was Jack Warner's decision to film the movie in black and white. The magical mood that Errol created in *The Adventures of Robin Hood* is somewhat lost, and perhaps one of the reasons Errol was again passed over for a best actor nomination. It was an unfortunate choice because the overall pomp and pageantry of the production, which also included the construction of two full sized pirate vessels. The entire production also featured many lavish locations and the cast donned numerous period costumes, all of which would have been tailor made for color.

The studio knew that they could cast Errol Flynn in the role of a Canadian Mounted Policeman, then add to the mix a German U-Boat, Nazis, a downed German Bomber they have to repair and a ski chase right out of a James Bond Movie. The result was one

Errol and his daughters

more unique action packed Errol Flynn adventure movie. The title of this saga was, *Northern Pursuit*. Errol was like a chameleon, he could change from being a pirate, to an outlaw in a forest, to a prize fighter and now a most believable hero in the Canadian wilderness. Several years later Errol Flynn was still at his peak and in his 31st Hollywood movie the studio decided to cast him in *The Adventures of Don Juan*. The year was 1948 and once again Errol Flynn proved he still was able to play a swashbuckler. The studio was fickle when it came to some of their productions, but for some strange reason even though Errol was never their favorite son they pulled out all the stops for *Don Juan*. The movie featured a lavish Max Steiner music score, Academy Award winning costumes and of course a stunning leading lady for Errol, Viveca Lindfors. One of Errol's buddies on and off the screen Alan Hale was also cast as Don Juan's sidekick. In *The Adventures of Don Juan*, it was evident from the very first scene that Errol could easily convince the audience of his never duplicated prowess with the opposite sex. Throughout the entire movie Errol's devil-may-care and unique persona were at their peak. Errol prove that he was also still able to pull off his own

Errol and wife Patrice Wymore

stunts and in one memorable scene Errol has a toss and tumble duel with no less than six adversaries. The movie was very well received by the public and even one *New York Times* critic wrote, "....a production of rare magnificence...something to remember old Hollywood and its true stars by..."

Fast forward to 1957, just two years before Errol Flynn's bright flame would burn out, and by chance Errol found himself cast in the Ernest Hemingway production of *The Sun Also Rises*. For the very last time in Errol's all too brief career, Errol stole the show and the hearts of the audience, exactly as he did decades ago in *Captain Blood*. It was no secret that Errol was not what Hollywood deemed a leading man anymore. For that reason Errol was billed behind Tyrone Power, Ava Gardner and Mel Ferrer, but it was Errol who lit up the screen as the hopeless alcoholic. The critics felt that it was merely Errol playing himself, this time without a sword or gun in his hand only a bottle as a prop. It wouldn't be fair to leave out still one more memorable performance. *They Died with Their Boots On* has been previously discussed, but *Rocky Mountain*, Errol's last

Errol and Patrice dancing at a function

cowboy movie, is also one of Errol's best. Even though it is another production shot in black-and-white, that fact adds to the gritty performance Errol turns in. This time Errol is a Confederate soldier and he aptly runs the gamut of emotions the role requires. Errol makes the audience in his own imitable style feel all the disappointment when his character has his goal to organize a Confederate militia is completely sidetracked as Errol is abandoned on a rocky mountain range. In a strange turn of events, Errol rescues a stagecoach from the Indians and alerts his enemies the Yankees, a masterful piece of acting Errol always pulled off with casual skill.

Errol, Patrice and their daughter

Errol and Patrice

Errol on his wedding day

Errol and Patrice in Cuba

Errol and his beloved son, Sean

Having fun with Patrice

A young Errol with Lili Damita

Errol and Lili on one of his boats

Kissing under the mistletoe

Sean, a father's joy

Turning back the clock once again to 1949, Errol surprised everyone including the critics when in still another unusual dramatic performance *That Forsyte Woman* was released. Errol was cast along with a who's who of Hollywood royalty, some of the greatest actors and actresses of that era. Opposite Errol was Walter Pidgeon, Robert Young and Greer Garson, but it was Errol who virtually walked away with the movie with his bravado performance as the hard headed, self-righteous Victorian bloat. It should be noted that this production was based on book number one of John Galsworthy's *The Forsyte Saga*. In recent times the updated version was featured on PBS' *Masterpiece Theatre* and it actually won numerous awards. The character that Errol played received one of the awards but Errol's portrayal of that character far outshines the updated one in not only a visual sense, but an artistic one.

The subject of war and war heroes and villains was still another perfect vehicle for Errol Flynn's range of acting attributes, his very natural ones. Errol starred in no less than half a dozen War movies. They were, *The Dawn Patrol, Desperate Journey, Edge of Darkness, Dive Bomber, Objective Burma,* and *Another Dawn.* In *Edge of Darkness,* Errol was at his best playing a straight dramatic role, staying in character as a serious and stern individual for the entire two hour saga. It was just another category of movie characters that most of the time required Errol to wear a uniform, wear it he did like no other actor before or since.

The journey is nearing a sad ending for the incomparable Errol Flynn, the year is now 1959, and that year 1959 was to be Errol's last. One of Errol's friends, a sort of washed up B movie producer, Barry Mahon, convinced Errol to star in a semi-documentary regarding Fidel Castro and his fight with Fulgencio Batista. Errol Flynn actually wrote the screenplay, narrated the film and starred as the main character. It was a testimony of how far from the spotlight Errol had distanced himself from the glamour of Hollywood. The black and white film ran only 68 minutes long and Errol's legacy in films would end with the production *Cuban Rebel Girls.*

It was a cold rainy Saturday when I decided to go to 42nd Street and see first-hand what had become of my hero. As I purchased my token on the 181st Street subway station, the clerk looked at me and smiled, as he handed me change for my dollar. I stopped in my tracks and did a double take, you see he had jet black hair and the signature pencil thin mustache that Errol Flynn had made so famous. The subway ride to 42nd Street was taking much longer then I had ever remembered and even though the train was almost empty for some strange reason I felt crowded in my seat and very uncomfortable. The whole day so far was filled with unusual happenings and I was overcome with these morbid feelings. Finally, the train screeched to a halt and there I was waiting for the dingy rusted subway doors to open and make my way to the air above the stench that was synonymous with the New York City subway system. The walk from the train station was a short one and I never owned or carried an umbrella in my life, but fortunately the rain had turned to a slight drizzle. If you have never been to 42nd Street here is what catches your eyes for the first time: movie marquees with thousands of blinking lights that advertise what's playing. Some are small and some are gigantic. The movie house I was headed to was a smaller one. As I approached the theater the marquee read "Errol Flynn" in big red letters and under his name was *Cuban Rebel Girls*. The poster of the movie on the promenade, as well as, the many black and white stills from *Cuban Rebel Girls* made me feel like something was missing. Unlike, *The Adventures of Robin Hood* which boasted a magnificent full color portrait of Errol, as well as, dynamic graphics, the poster of *Cuban Rebel Girls* was a poor pencil like sketch. The black and white photos were not very clear and were more like vacation photographs than scenes from a motion picture. When I finally got to my seat the interior of the old run down theater was almost empty. There were about seven or eight people including myself and some looked like they had slept in the movie house the night before. The movie began and it was evident from the opening credits and the music that accompanied them this was not a Wolfgang Korngold score. As the action started, the movie began almost as if it was a travel log of sorts and you could say without conviction the photography was shabby at best. Errol Flynn looked very tired and was a shell of the dynamic hero that lit up the screen for over two decades. The movie was over before I realized it had begun. It was a snapshot of a dramatic ending of a dramatic career. I almost forgot the year was 1959 and you never saw one movie, the first feature that was shown on this double bill before Errol Flynn's very last movie was shown had the very appropriate title *The Beast from the Haunted Cave.*

Ever since that very unique and faithful day when I was fortunate to see Errol Flynn for the very first time on the big screen in *The Adventures of Robin Hood*, it seems the journey has gone full circle as he ended up somewhere in Cuba. It was for me, a very sad ending as the credits rolled for *Cuban Rebel Girls*. As the screen went blank and the few patrons lumbered up the dingy lit movie theater isles, I sat in a dreamlike state. My mind was wandering and I envisioned Errol in Sherwood Forest, one more time, on a pirate ship or being held in some beautiful starlet's arms as he kissed her, but only this time it was really for the last time.

I only hope that after reading this account of the many reasons why Errol Flynn truly deserves an Oscar, you, the reader will take the time to seek out his unique body of work in film. Then after making your own conclusions, once again I am convinced you will whole heartedly agree he was deserving of Hollywood's greatest prize, you can almost hear Errol saying, "Welcome to Sherwood Forest."

CHAPTER 8:
Short Interesting Facts

- Errol Flynn was married three times, and had four children:
    - ❖ Lili Damita from 1935 until 1942
        - ◆ one son, Sean Flynn, born 1941, reported missing in Cambodia in 1970 and presumed dead
    - ❖ Nora Eddington from 1943 until 1949
        - ◆ two daughters, Deirdre born 1945 and Rory born 1947
    - ❖ Patrice Wymore from 1950 until his death
        - ◆ one daughter, Arnella Roma, 1953–1998

- Errol had many boats, his favorite boats were:
    - ❖ *Zaca*
    - ❖ *Sirocco*

- One of Errol Flynn's favorite ports of sea was:
    - ❖ Port in Antonio, in Jamaica. Today a beautiful marina bears his name. The Errol Flynn Marina Port Antonio, Jamaica, is located adjacent to his plantation-like house on the magnificent Caribbean island.

- Errol Flynn wrote three books, two of which were novels, *Beam Ends* and *Showdown*, the third was an autobiography, *My Wicked, Wicked Ways*.

- Today, over 50 years after Errol Flynn's death, there are modern trading cards that have actual pieces of his clothes attached (see photo), and one company in Europe has issued a Robin Hood model kit (see photo).

- Of course Errol Flynn has a star on the Hollywood Walk of Fame, the location is 7008 Hollywood Blvd, Los Angeles.

- Turner Classic Movie channel frequently airs tribute days in honor of his many great movies. Robert Osborne, the renowned film historian, considers Errol Flynn's rendition of *The Adventures of Robin Hood* as the best Robin Hood version.

- There are also several unique box sets of Errol Flynn movies that have been released by Turner Classic Movies.

- Errol Flynn has been chosen as the greatest pirate of all time. Swashbuckler Errol Flynn was picked over Johnny Depp by winning Hollywood's top Buccaneer title in a New World Entertainment News Network (WENN) poll. WENN editors teamed up with the renowned British Buccaneer buff David Cordingley, a consultant on the first *Pirates of the Caribbean* movie, to scour the movie seven seas to come up with the definitive movie pirates poll. The expert has chosen Errol Flynn's Captain Blood as the pick of the pirates, ahead of Johnny Depp's Captain Jack Sparrow. Some of the accolades describe Errol as having much more charisma, more good looks and is physically convincing. It was also noted in the review that Errol Flynn really did fence in all of the fencing scenes in *Captain Blood*; a stunt double was never used.

French poster of *Adventures of Don Juan*

Italian poster of *Adventures of Don Juan*

Italian poster of *Captain Blood*

Italian poster of *San Antonio*

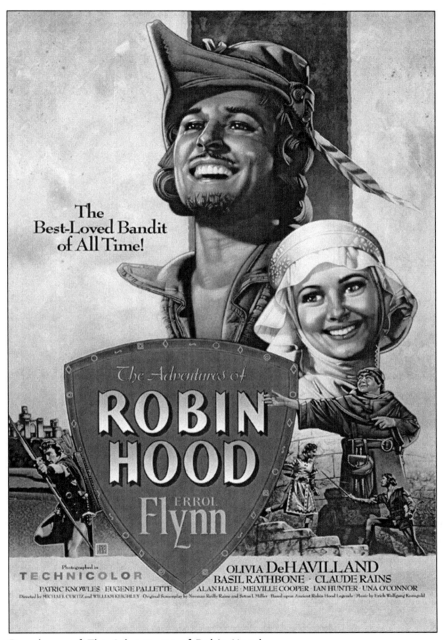

Re-release of *The Adventures of Robin Hood*

German poster of *Escape Me Never*

Alternate poster of *Another Dawn*

Lobby card of *Northern Pursuit*

German program of *The Adventures of Robin Hood*

Austrian program of *The Charge of The Light Brigade*

German program of *Rocky Mountain*

German program of *The Charge of The Light Brigade*

German program of *Adventures of Don Juan*

German program of *Against All Flags*

German program of *The Private Lives of Elizabeth and Essex*

German program of *The Sea Hawk*

Rare magazine advertisement of *Against All Flags*, 1952

German program of *Objective Burma*

Comic book of *Montana*

Rare resin figure of Robin Hood

German stamp of Robin Hood

Current day trading card which includes an actual piece of Errol's clothing

Movie Mirror magazine

Picture Play movie magazine

Screen Romances magazine

Rare British artwork used for series of video tapes released in England

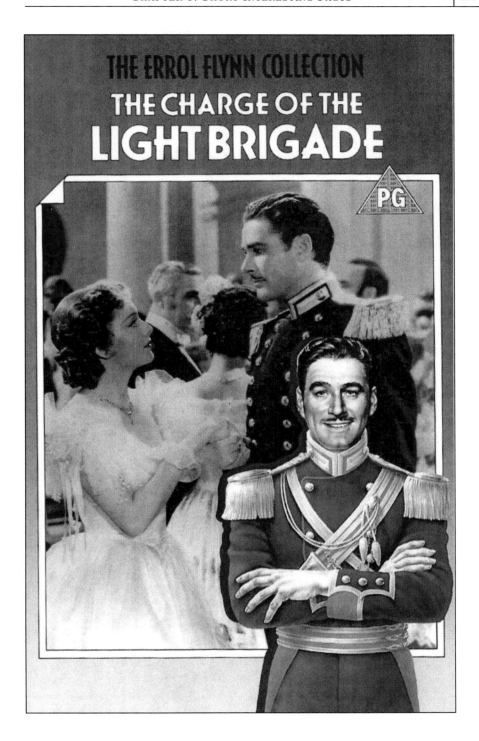

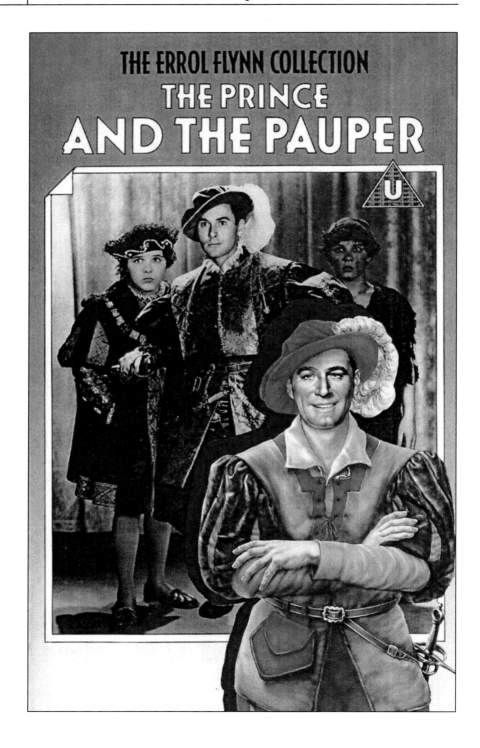

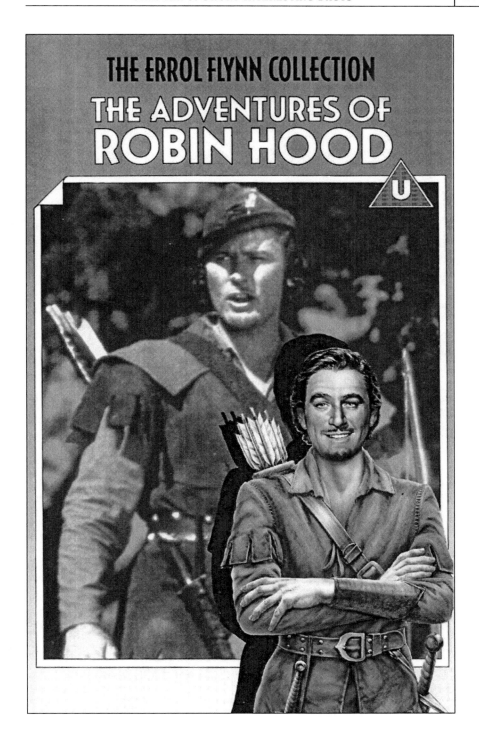

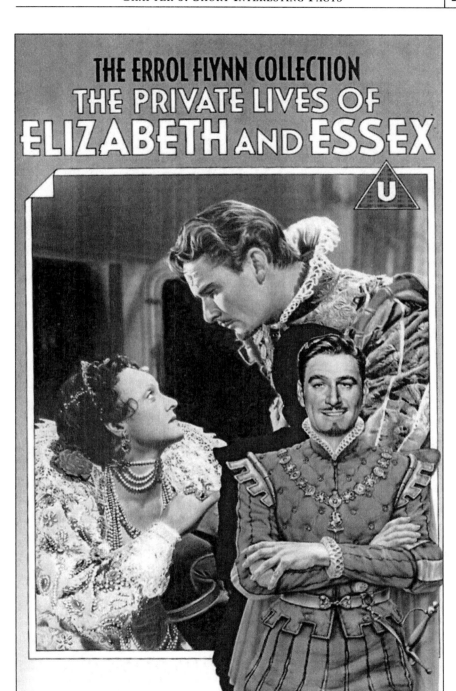

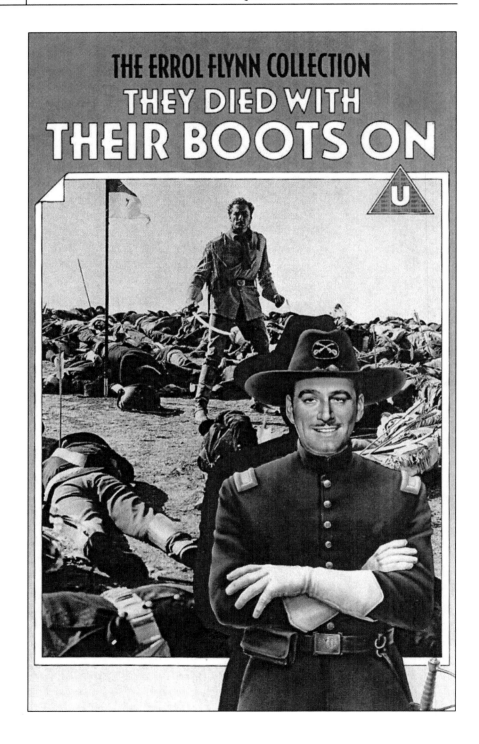

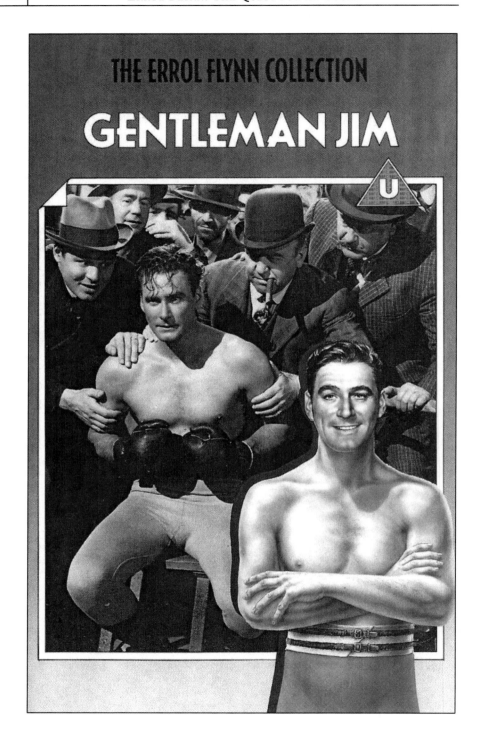

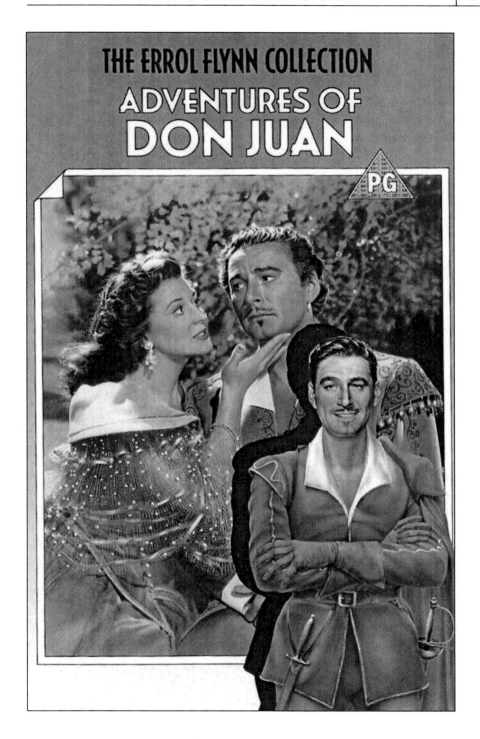

CHAPTER 9:
Quotes

"He was a charming and magnetic man, but so tormented. I don't know about what, but tormented."

— Olivia de Havilland, actress

"He was all the heroes in one magnificent, sexy, animal package. I just wish we had someone around today half as good as Flynn."

— Jack L. Warner, studio boss

"He was an enchanting creature. I had more fun with Errol than everybody else put together…It was never ending fun."

— David Niven, friend and actor

"Errol had the capacity to make everything an adventure—Even a quiet stroll through a simple country lane came alive either through a quick remembrance or a philosophical thought or a simple observation of the ecological patterns of the earth trees and flowers and their support system. His was a mind relentlessly searching."

— Patrice Wymore Flynn, wife

"He was one of the most poetic men I have ever met, and he could describe trees and flowers and the wonders of the ocean in the most beautiful language."

— Earl Conrad, journalist of Flynn's autobiography

"He was one of the wild characters of the world, but he also had a strange, quiet side. He camouflaged himself completely. In all the years I knew him, I never knew what really lay underneath, and I doubt if many people did."

— Ann Sheridan, actress

"He had the charm of a mischievous small boy, humorous and impossible to dislike."

— Arthur Hiller, director

"I loved him anyway and he was, as everyone suspected, an endearing rascal."

— Lili Damita, first wife

"The only time he wasn't living was when he was asleep, and even then I think he dreamt well."

— Nora Haymes, second wife

CHAPTER 10:
The Movies of Errol Flynn

"They've great respect for the dead in Hollywood,
but none for the living."

ADVENTURES OF CAPTAIN FABIAN 1951 N/R, 100 MIN.

GENRE: ADVENTURE
DIRECTOR: WILLIAM MARSHALL
CAST: ERROL FLYNN, MICHELINE PRESLE, AGNES
            MOOREHEAD, VINCENT PRICE, VICTOR FRANCEN,
            REGGIE NALDER, JIM GERALD, HELENA MANSON,
            HOWARD VERNON, MARCEL JOURNET, ROGER
            BLIN, VALENTINE CAMAX, GEORGES FLATEAU,
            ZANIE CAMPAN, REGGIE NALDER

Errol Flynn portrays swashbuckling sea captain Fabian who becomes involved with servant girl Lea Marriote (Micheline Presle). Lea marries George Brissac (Vincent Price) who talks her into murdering his uncle so that he can obtain the family money. Fabian is accused of the murder but escapes with Lea who is killed during the escape, and Fabian sails away.

CAST

ERROL FLYNN	CAPT. MICHAEL FABIAN
MICHELINE PRESLE	LEA MARIOTTE
AGNES MOOREHEAD	AUNT JEZEBEL
VINCENT PRICE	GEORGE BRISSAC
VICTOR FRANCEN	HENRI BRISSAC
REGGIE NALDER	CONSTANT
JIM GERALD	COMMISSIONER GERMAIN
HELENA MANSON	JOSEPHINE

HOWARD VERNON	EMILE
ROGER BLIN	PHILIPPE
VALENTINE CAMAX	GOVERNESS
GEORGES FLATEAU	JUDGE JEAN BRISSAC
ZANIE CAMPAN	CYNTHIA WINTROP
REGGIE NALDER	CONSTANT

ADVENTURES OF DON JUAN 1948 N/R, 110 MIN.

GENRE:	ADVENTURE/ACTION/ROMANCE
DIRECTOR:	VINCENT SHERMAN
CAST:	ERROL FLYNN, VIVECA LINDFORS, ROBERT DOUGLAS, ALAN HALE, ANN RUTHERFORD, RAYMOND BURR, HELEN WESTCOTT, DOUGLAS KENNEDY, UNA O'CONNOR, ROBERT WARWICK, ROMNEY BRENT, JERRY AUSTIN, JEAN SHEPHERD, FORTUNIO BONANOVA, AUBREY MATHER

Errol Flynn, in his last epic adventure, excels in his role of the famous lover, Don Juan. After Don Juan's indiscreet womanizing, in an attempt to rehabilitate him, Queen Margaret (Viveca Lindfors) offers him the position of fencing instructor at the royal fencing academy. While there, Don Juan learns that the evil Duke de Loerea (Robert Douglas) is plotting to take over the throne, and—aided by Leporello (Alan Hale), Don Serafino (Fortunio Bonanova), and Don Sebastian (Jerry Austin)—Don Juan foils the plans. The film won an Academy Award for Best Costumes.

CAST

ERROL FLYNN	DON JUAN DE MACANA
VIVECA LINDFORS	QUEEN MARGARET
ROBERT DOUGLAS	DUKE DE LORCA
ALAN HALE	LEPORELLO
ANN RUTHERFORD	DONNA ELENA
RAYMOND BURR	CAPTAIN ALVAREZ
HELEN WESTCOTT	LADY DIANA
DOUGLAS KENNEDY	DON RODRIGO

UNA O'CONNOR	DUENNA
ROBERT WARWICK	DON JOSE—COUNT DE POLAN
ROMNEY BRENT	KING PHILLIP III
JERRY AUSTIN	DON SEBASTIAN
JEAN SHEPHERD	DONNA CARLOTTA
FORTUNIO BONANOVA	DON SERAFINO LOPEZ
AUBREY MATHER	LORD CHALMERS

THE ADVENTURES OF ROBIN HOOD 1938 N/R, 106 MIN.

GENRE:	ACTION/ADVENTURE/ROMANCE
DIRECTOR:	MICHAEL CURTIZ, WILLIAM KEIGHLEY
CAST:	ERROL FLYNN, BASIL RATHBONE, IAN HUNTER, OLIVIA DE HAVILLAND, CLAUDE RAINS, PATRIC KNOWLES, EUGENE PALLETTE, ALAN HALE, MELVILLE COOPER, UNA O'CONNOR, HERBERT MUNDIN, MONTAGU LOVE, ROBERT NOBLE, LEONARD WILLEY, KENNETH HUNTER

Errol Flynn IS Robin Hood. Romance blooms between Robin and Maid Marian (Olivia de Havilland) in the midst of sweeping sword fights in Sherwood Forest as Robin leads his band of merry men against Prince John (Claude Rains) and his efforts to tax the poor. The film received an Oscar nomination for Best Picture.

CAST

ERROL FLYNN	ROBIN HOOD
BASIL RATHBONE	SIR GUY OF GISBOURNE
IAN HUNTER	KING RICHARD THE LION HEARTED
OLIVIA DE HAVILLAND	MAID MARIAN
CLAUDE RAINS	PRINCE JOHN
PATRIC KNOWLES	WILL SCARLETT
EUGENE PALLETTE	FRIAR TUCK
ALAN HALE	LITTLE JOHN
MELVILLE COOPER	HIGH SHERIFF OF NOTTINGHAM
UNA O'CONNOR	BESS
HERBERT MUNDIN	MUCH-THE-MILLER'S-SON

MONTAGU LOVE	BISHOP OF THE BLACK CANONS
ROBERT NOBLE	SIR RALF
LEONARD WILLEY	SIR ESSEX
KENNETH HUNTER	SIR MORTIMER

AGAINST ALL FLAGS 1952 N/R, 83 MIN.

GENRE:	ADVENTURE/ACTION/ DRAMA
DIRECTOR:	GEORGE SHERMAN
CAST:	ERROL FLYNN, MAUREEN O'HARA, ANTHONY QUINN, ALICE KELLEY, MILDRED NATWICK, ROBERT WARWICK, HARRY CORDING, PHIL TULLY, LESTER MATTHEWS, JOHN ALDERSON, TUDOR OWEN, MAURICE MARSAC, JAMES CRAVEN, JAMES FAIRFAX, JAMES LOGAN

During the 16th century, swashbuckling British naval officer Brian Hawke (Errol Flynn) goes undercover and manages to enter a pirate fortress on Madagascar. His mission is to learn more about Capt. Roc Brasiliano (Anthony Quinn) whose pirate band is attacking ships. Problems ensue, and Brasiliano demands that Hawke be executed, but pirate Spitfire Stevens (Maureen O'Hara) defends Hawke. During a raid on an Indian ship, Princess Patma (Alice Kelley) is kidnapped, but Hawke gets the information he needs on the pirate activities, rescues Princess Patma, and escapes the pirates. This film was remade in 1967 as *The King's Pirate* with Doug McClure in Flynn's role.

CAST

ERROL FLYNN	BRIAN HAWKE
MAUREEN O'HARA	PRUDENCE "SPITFIRE" STEVENS
ANTHONY QUINN	CAPT. ROC BRASILIANO
ALICE KELLEY	PRINCESS PATMA
MILDRED NATWICK	MOLVINA MACGREGOR
ROBERT WARWICK	CAPT. KIDD
HARRY CORDING	GOW
PHIL TULLY	JONES

LESTER MATTHEWS	SIR CLOUDSLEY
JOHN ALDERSON	JONATHAN HARRIS
TUDOR OWEN	WILLIAMS
MAURICE MARSAC	CAPT. MOISSON
JAMES CRAVEN	CAPT. HORNSBY
JAMES FAIRFAX	CRUIKSHANK
JAMES LOGAN	CAPT. ROBERTS

ALWAYS TOGETHER 1948 N/R, 78 MIN.

GENRE:	COMEDY
DIRECTOR:	FREDERICK DE CORDOVA
CAST:	ROBERT HUTTON, JOYCE REYNOLDS, CECIL KELLAWAY, ERNEST TRUEX, HUMPHREY BOGART, JACK CARSON, ALEXIS SMITH, ERROL FLYNN, JANIS PAIGE, DENNIS MORGAN, DON MCGUIRE, RANSOM M. SHERMAN, DOUGLAS KENNEDY, BARBARA BATES, RALPH BROOKS

Jane Barker (Joyce Reynolds) inherits $1,000,000 when millionaire Jonathan Turner (Cecil Kellaway) believes that he is dying. Just when Jane and her husband Donn (Robert Hutton) begin plans to enjoy their newfound wealth, the benefactor recovers—and wants his $1,000,000 back! Throughout her problems, Jane imagines that her experiences are movies, and real actors are part of her imagination.

CAST

ROBERT HUTTON	DONN MASTERS
JOYCE REYNOLDS	JANE BARKER
CECIL KELLAWAY	JONATHAN TURNER
ERNEST TRUEX	MR. TIMOTHY J. BULL
HUMPHREY BOGART	HIMSELF
JACK CARSON	HIMSELF
ALEXIS SMITH	HERSELF
ERROL FLYNN	HIMSELF
JANIS PAIGE	HERSELF
DENNIS MORGAN	HIMSELF

DON MCGUIRE	MCINTYRE
RANSOM M. SHERMAN	JUDGE
DOUGLAS KENNEDY	DOBERMAN
BARBARA BATES	TICKET SELLER
RALPH BROOKS	REPORTER

ANOTHER DAWN 1937 N/R, 73 MIN.

GENRE:	ADVENTURE/DRAMA/ROMANCE
DIRECTOR:	WILLIAM DIETERLE
CAST:	KAY FRANCIS, ERROL FLYNN, IAN HUNTER, FRIEDA INESCORT, MARY FORBES, HERBERT MUNDIN, BILLY BEVAN, KENNETH HUNTER, CLYDE COOK, CHARLES IRWIN, G.P. HUNTLEY, RICHARD POWELL, EILY MALYON, DAVID CLYDE, SPENCER TEAKLE

In this story set in Africa, Captain Denny Roark (Errol Flynn) is grieving over the death of his lover when he falls in love with Julia Ashton (Kay Francis), the wife of his commanding officer, Colonel Wister (Ian Hunter). When the war with the African tribes heats up, Wister volunteers for a suicide mission, and Denny and Julia continue their love affair.

CAST

KAY FRANCIS	JULIA ASHTON WISTER
ERROL FLYNN	CAPTAIN DENNY ROARK
IAN HUNTER	COLONEL JOHN WISTER
FRIEDA INESCORT	GRACE ROARK
MARY FORBES	MRS. LYDIA BENTON
HERBERT MUNDIN	WILKINS
BILLY BEVAN	PVT. HAWKINS
KENNETH HUNTER	SIR CHAS. BENTON
CLYDE COOK	SERGEANT MURPHY
CHARLES IRWIN	KELLY
G.P. HUNTLEY	LORD ALDEN
RICHARD POWELL	PVT. HENDERSON

EILY MALYON   MRS. FARNOLD
DAVID CLYDE   CAMPBELL
SPENCER TEAKLE   FROMBY

THE BIG BOODLE 1957 N/R, 83 MIN.

GENRE: DRAMA/THRILLER
DIRECTOR: RICHARD WILSON
CAST: ERROL FLYNN, PEDRO ARMENDARIZ, ROSANNA
            RORY, GIA SCALA, JACQUES AUBUCHON,
            FRANCISCO CANERO, LUIS OQUENDO

In pre-Castro Cuba, a Casino blackjack dealer (Errol Flynn) finds plates belonging to counterfeiters, and the discovery begins his trek into Havana's underworld.

CAPTAIN BLOOD 1935 N/R, 119 MIN.

GENRE: ADVENTURE
DIRECTOR: MICHAEL CURTIZ
CAST: ERROL FLYNN, OLIVIA DE HAVILLAND, BASIL
            RATHBONE, LIONEL ATWILL, ROSS ALEXANDER,
            GUY KIBBEE, HENRY STEPHENSON, DONALD MEEK,
            J. CARROL NAISH, HOBART CAVANAUGH

This film represents the first teaming of Errol Flynn and Olivia de Havilland and made them both stars. Surgeon Peter Blood (Errol Flynn) rebels against England's James II who deports him as a slave to the West Indies where he is purchased by Colonel Bishop (Lionel Atwill). Set free, Blood falls in love with Bishop's niece, Arabella (Olivia de Havilland), and he turns to piracy as part of his fight against slavery. This Hal Wallis film was nominated for an Oscar.

THE CASE OF THE CURIOUS BRIDE 1935 N/R, 74 MIN.

GENRE: MYSTERY
DIRECTOR: MICHAEL CURTIZ
CAST: WARREN WILLIAM, MARGARET LINDSAY,
            DONALD WOODS, CLAIRE DODD, ALLEN JENKINS,
            PHILLIP REED, WINI SHAW, ERROL FLYNN

Humor underlies this Perry Mason case of a woman who says she is being blackmailed by her husband.

THE CHARGE OF THE LIGHT BRIGADE 1936 N/R, 115 MIN.

GENRE: ACTION/DRAMA/ADVENTURE/ROMANCE
DIRECTOR: MICHAEL CURTIZ
CAST: ERROL FLYNN, OLIVIA DE HAVILLAND,
            PATRIC KNOWLES, DONALD CRISP, NIGEL BRUCE,
            HENRY STEPHENSON, DAVID NIVEN, SPRING
            BYINGTON, J. CARROL NAISH, E.E. CLIVE,
            C. HENRY GORDON, G.P. HUNTLEY, ROBERT
            BARRAT, WALTER HOLBROOK, SCOTTY BECKETT

In this film version of Alfred Lord Tennyson's poem, set during the 1854 Crimean War, Major Geoffrey Vickers (Errol Flynn) vows revenge on the Indian potentate Surat Khan (C. Henry Gordon) after witnessing a slaughter of British citizens at a British fort commanded by Col. Campbell (Donald Crisp). Meanwhile, Geoffrey and his brother Perry (Patric Knowles), who is also a soldier, are both in love with Campbell's daughter Elsa (Olivia de Havilland), but it is Perry who wins her heart. Now, Geoffrey leads his Light Brigade into a fight to the death against the Russian soldiers who are providing supplies to Surat Khan.

CAST

ERROL FLYNN	MAJOR GEOFFREY VICKERS
OLIVIA DE HAVILLAND	ELSA CAMPBELL
PATRIC KNOWLES	CAPTAIN PERRY VICKERS

DONALD CRISP	COLONEL CAMPBELL
NIGEL BRUCE	SIR BENJAMIN WARRENTON
HENRY STEPHENSON	SIR CHARLES MACEFIELD
DAVID NIVEN	CAPTAIN JAMES RANDALL
SPRING BYINGTON	LADY OCTAVIA WARRENTON
J. CARROL NAISH	SUBAHDAR-MAJOR PURAN SINGH
E.E. CLIVE	SIR HUMPHREY HARCOURT
C. HENRY GORDON	SURAT KHAN
G.P. HUNTLEY	MAJOR JOWETT
ROBERT BARRAT	COUNT IGOR VOLONOFF
WALTER HOLBROOK	COMET CHARLES BARCLAY
SCOTTY BECKETT	PREMA SINGH

CROSSED SWORDS 1954 N/R, 83 MIN.

GENRE: ADVENTURE
DIRECTOR: MILTON KRIMS
CAST: ERROL FLYNN, GINA LOLLOBRIGIDA,
            CESARE DANOVA, NADIA GRAY, ROLDANO LUPI,
            RICCARDO RIOLI, ALBERTO RABAGLIATI, PAOLA
            MORI, SILVIO BAGOLINI, RENATO CHIANTONI,
            PIETRO TORDI, ALFREDO RIZZO

Adventurer Renzo (Errol Flynn) fights against an evil plot to oust the Duke of Sidona (Pietro Tordi) from the Italian court, and, in his spare time, Renzo romances the Duke's daughter (Gina Lollobrigida) who assures him that marriage will not end his world of swash-buckling.

CRY WOLF 1947 N/R, 83 MIN.

GENRE: MYSTERY
DIRECTOR: PETER GODFREY
CAST: ERROL FLYNN, BARBARA STANWYCK, GERALDINE
            BROOKS, RICHARD BASEHART, JEROME COWAN,
            JOHN RIDGELY, PATRICIA BARRY, JACK MOWER,

PAUL STANTON, RORY MALLINSON, HELEN
THIMIG, BARRY BERNARD, JOHN ELLIOTT,
CREIGHTON HALE, LISA GOLM

Sandra Marshall (Barbara Stanwyck) returns to her late husband
James' family mansion for his funeral and announces to James'
research scientist uncle, Mark (Errol Flynn), the news of her secret
marriage to James. Mark distrusts Sandra but allows her to stay at the
mansion, where she makes friends with James' sister Julie (Geraldine
Brooks), who then dies under mysterious circumstances. Sandra
believes that Mark has committed the murder of Julie, but are her
suspicions correct?

CAST

ERROL FLYNN	MARK CALDWELL
BARBARA STANWYCK	SANDRA MARSHALL
GERALDINE BROOKS	JULIE DEMAREST
RICHARD BASEHART	JAMES CALDWELL DEMAREST
JEROME COWAN	SEN. CHARLES CALDEWLL
JOHN RIDGELY	JACKSON LEIDELL
PATRICIA BARRY	ANGELA THE MAID
JACK MOWER	WATKINS
PAUL STANTON	DAVENPORT
RORY MALLINSON	BECKET THE BUTLER
HELEN THIMIG	MARTA THE HOUSEKEEPER
BARRY BERNARD	ROBERTS
JOHN ELLIOTT	CLERGYMAN (VOICE)
CREIGHTON HALE	DR. REYNOLDS
LISA GOLM	MRS. LAIDELL

CUBAN REBEL GIRLS 1959 N/R, 68 MIN.

GENRE:	ACTION/ADVENTURE
AKA:	ASSAULT OF THE REBEL GIRLS
	ATTACK OF THE REBEL GIRLS
DIRECTOR:	BARRY MAHON
CAST:	ERROL FLYNN, BEVERLY AADLAND, JOHN MACKAY,

MARIE EDMUND, JACKIE JACKLER, CLELLE
MAHON, BEN OSTROWSKY, TOD SCOTT BRODY,
RAMON RAMIEREZ, REYNERIO SANCHEZ, ANDRES
FERNANDEZ, ESTHER OLIVA, ALLEN BARON

During Fidel Castro's revolution against Fulgencio Batista, Cuban
women plot to smuggle weapons to the rebels with the help of Errol
Flynn who plays himself as a war correspondent.

CAST

ERROL FLYNN	AMERICAN CORRESPONDENT
BEVERLY AADLAND	BEVERLY WOODS
JOHN MACKAY	REBEL CAPT. JOHNNY WILSON
MARIE EDMUND	MARIA RODRIGUEZ
JACKIE JACKLER	JACQUELINE DOMINGUEZ
BEN OSTROWSKY	RAOUL "BEN" DOMINGUEZ
TOD SCOTT BRODY	TODD

THE DARK AVENGER 1955 N/R, 85 MIN.

GENRE:	ACTION
AKA:	THE WARRIORS
DIRECTOR:	HENRY LEVIN
CAST:	ERROL FLYNN, JOANNE DRU, PETER FINCH, YVONNE FURNEAUX, PATRICK HOLT, MICHAEL HORDERN, CHRISTOPHER LEE, SAM KYDD, ROBERT URQUHART, MOULTRIE KELSALL

Prince Edward (Errol Flynn) rescues Lady Joan Holland (Joanne
Dru) and her children from the clutches of the diabolical Count De
Ville (Peter Finch).

THE DAWN PATROL 1938 N/R, 103 MIN.

GENRE: ACTION/DRAMA/ADVENTURE
DIRECTOR: EDMUND GOULDING
CAST: ERROL FLYNN, BASIL RATHBONE, DAVID NIVEN,
            BARRY FITZGERALD, DONALD CRISP, MELVILLE
            COOPER, CARL ESMOND, PETER WILLES,
            MORTON LOWRY, MICHAEL BROOKE, HERBERT
            EVANS, JAMES BURKE, STUART HALL, SIDNEY
            BRACEY, LEO NOMIS

In this remake of the 1930 film, Basil Rathbone plays the squadron commander, Major Brand, who must send young British World War I aviators to their possible deaths. Flight commander, Capt. Courtney (Errol Flynn) leads his men on their fatal missions and resents Brand's ruthlessness in sending them to their deaths. But, when Courtney replaces Brand as squadron commander, he is the one blamed— until he performs a suicidal bombing mission and is killed. Now, the cycle continues when Courtney's best friend, Lt. Scott (David Niven), becomes squadron commander and must deal with taking the blame.

CAST

ERROL FLYNN	CAPTAIN COURTNEY
BASIL RATHBONE	MAJOR BRAND
DAVID NIVEN	LIEUTENANT SCOTT
BARRY FITZGERALD	BOTT
DONALD CRISP	PHIPPS
MELVILLE COOPER	SERGEANT WATKINS
CARL ESMOND	VON MUELLER
PETER WILLES	HOLLISTER
MORTON LOWRY	DONNIE SCOTT
MICHAEL BROOKE	CAPTAIN SQUIRES
HERBERT EVANS	SCOTT'S MECHANIC
JAMES BURKE	FLAHERTY
STUART HALL	BENTHAM
SIDNEY BRACEY	MAJOR BRAND'S ORDERLY
LEO NOMIS	AERONAUTIC SUPERVISOR

DESPERATE JOURNEY 1942 N/R, 107 MIN.

GENRE: DRAMA
DIRECTOR: RAOUL WALSH
CAST: ERROL FLYNN, RONALD REAGAN, RAYMOND
             MASSEY, NANCY COLEMAN, ALAN HALE, ARTHUR
             KENNEDY, SIG RUMAN, PATRICK O'MOORE,
             CHARLES IRWIN, RICHARD FRASER, RONALD
             SINCLAIR, ALBERT BASSERMAN, FELIX BASCH,
             ILKA GRUNING, ELSA BASSERMAN

World War II airmen—Lt. Terrence Forbes (Errol Flynn) and his men Johnny Hammond (Ronald Reagan), Kirk Edwards (Alan Hale), Jed Forrest (Arthur Kennedy), and Lloyd Hollis (Ronald Sinclair)—survive a crash behind enemy lines in Poland and set out to find their way back to England. Pursued by Nazi Major Otto Baumeister (Raymond Massey), they find their means of escape when they steal a German plane and fly home to England.

CAST

ERROL FLYNN	FLIGHT LT. "TERRY" FORBES
RONALD REAGAN	FLYING OFFICER JOHNNY HAMMOND
RAYMOND MASSEY	MAJOR OTTO BAUMEISTER
NANCY COLEMAN	KAETHE BRAHMS
ALAN HALE	FLIGHT SERGEANT KIRK EDWARDS
ARTHUR KENNEDY	FLYING OFFICER JED FORREST
SIG RUMAN	PREUSS
PATRICK O'MOORE	SQUADRON LEADER LANE-FERRIS
CHARLES IRWIN	CAPTAIN COSWICK
RICHARD FRASER	SQUADRON LEADER CLARK
RONALD SINCLAIR	FLIGHT SERGEANT LLOYD HOLLIS
ALBERT BASSERMAN	DR. MATHER
FELIX BASCH	HERMANN BRAHMS
ILKA GRUNING	FRAU BRAHMS
ELSA BASSERMAN	FRAU RAEDER

DIVE BOMBER 1941 N/R, 130 MIN.

GENRE: ADVENTURE
DIRECTOR: MICHAEL CURTIZ
CAST: ERROL FLYNN, FRED MACMURRAY, RALPH
           BELLAMY, REGIS TOOMEY, CRAIG STEVENS,
           ROBERT ARMSTRONG, ALLEN JENKINS, ALEXIS
           SMITH, HERBERT ANDERSON, MORONI OLSEN

In pre-Pearl Harbor bombing days, scientist Doug Lee (Errol Flynn) tries to solve the problem of blackouts suffered by pilots training for possible future air battles.

DODGE CITY 1939 N/R, 100 MIN.

GENRE: WESTERN/ROMANCE
DIRECTOR: MICHAEL CURTIZ
CAST: ERROL FLYNN, OLIVIA DE HAVILLAND, ANN
           SHERIDAN, BRUCE CABOT, FRANK MCHUGH,
           ALAN HALE, JOHN LITEL, VICTOR JORY,
           GUINN "BIG BOY" WILLIAMS, WARD BOND,
           HENRY TRAVERS, HENRY O'NEILL, GLORIA
           HOLDEN, BOBS WATSON, DOUGLAS FOWLEY

A cattle man, Wade Hatton (Errol Flynn), arrives in Dodge City in 1872 and is appointed sheriff. He tries to tame Dodge City and must diminish the influences of outlaw saloon owner Jeff Surrett (Bruce Cabot) to obtain legitimacy for business interests and citizens in the town. Hatton manages to clean up Dodge City, and, in the process, wins the heart of Abbie Irving (Olivia de Havilland).

CAST

ERROL FLYNN	WADE HATTON
OLIVIA DE HAVILLAND	ABBIE IRVING
ANN SHERIDAN	RUBY GILMAN
BRUCE CABOT	JEFF SURRETT
FRANK MCHUGH	JOE CLEMENS

ALAN HALE	RUSTY HART
JOHN LITEL	MATT COLE
VICTOR JORY	YANCEY
GUINN "BIG BOY" WILLIAMS	TEX BAIRD
WARD BOND	BUD TAYLOR
HENRY TRAVERS	DR. IRVING
HENRY O'NEILL	COL. DODGE
GLORIA HOLDEN	MRS. COLE
BOBS WATSON	HARRY COLE
DOUGLAS FOWLEY	MUNGER

EDGE OF DARKNESS 1943 N/R, 120 MIN.

GENRE:	DRAMA
DIRECTOR:	LEWIS MILESTONE
CAST:	ERROL FLYNN, ANN SHERIDAN, WALTER HUSTON, NANCY COLEMAN, JUDITH ANDERSON, HELMUT DANTINE, RUTH GORDON, CHARLES DINGLE, JOHN BEAL, MONTE BLUE, MORRIS CARNOVSKY, ROMAN BOHNEN, RICHARD FRASER, ART SMITH, DOROTHY TREE

During World War II, the Nazis have invaded Norway, and the residents of the village of Trollness are living under the control of the cruel German Captain Hauptmann Kaunig (Helmut Dantine). The villagers are waiting for the British to deliver arms to aid in their resistance movement, which is led by Gunnar Brogge (Errol Flynn). Gunnar is aided by his fiancée, Karen Stensgard (Ann Sheridan), whose father, Martin (Walter Huston), is the town physician. However, the town is divided on how to handle the situation, and Gunnar and Karen know that their job will not be easy.

CAST

ERROL FLYNN	GUNNAR BROGGE
ANN SHERIDAN	KAREN STENSGARD
WALTER HUSTON	DR. MARTIN STENSGARD
NANCY COLEMAN	KATJA

JUDITH ANDERSON	GERD BJARNESEN
HELMUT DANTINE	CAPTAIN HAUPTMANN KOENIG
RUTH GORDON	ANNA STENSGARD
CHARLES DINGLE	KASPAR TORGERSON
JOHN BEAL	JOHANN STENSGARD
MONTE BLUE	PETERSEN
MORRIS CARNOVSKY	SIXTUS ANDRESEN
ROMAN BOHNEN	LARS MALKEN
RICHARD FRASER	PASTOR AALESEN
ART SMITH	KNUT OSTERHOLM
DOROTHY TREE	SOLVEIG BRATEGAARD

ESCAPE ME NEVER 1947 N/R, 104 MIN.

GENRE:	DRAMA
DIRECTOR:	PETER GODFREY
CAST:	ERROL FLYNN, IDA LUPINO, ELEANOR PARKER, GIG YOUNG, REGINALD DENNY, ISOBEL ELSOM, FRANK PUGLIA

Gemma Smith (Ida Lupino) is a poor widow who falls in love with a struggling musician. Problems develop following their marriage when he is attracted to a wealthy woman whose money will put an end to his dire financial situation.

FOOTSTEPS IN THE DARK 1941 N/R, 96 MIN.

GENRE:	COMEDY
DIRECTOR:	LLOYD BACON
CAST:	ERROL FLYNN, BRENDA MARSHALL, RALPH BELLAMY, ALAN HALE, LEE PATRICK, ALLEN JENKINS, LUCILE WATSON, WILLIAM FRAWLEY, ROSCOE KARNS, GRANT MITCHELL

While looking for ideas for crime novels, writer Francis Warren (Errol Flynn) heads for the seamy side of the city and ends up solving a real crime.

FOUR'S A CROWD 1938 N/R, 91 MIN.

GENRE: COMEDY
DIRECTOR: MICHAEL CURTIZ
CAST: ERROL FLYNN, OLIVIA DE HAVILLAND, ROSALIND
            RUSSELL, PATRIC KNOWLES, HUGH HERBERT,
            WALTER CONNOLLY, MELVILLE COOPER, FRANKLIN
            PANGBORN, HERMAN BING, MARGARET HAMILTON

A romantic triangle involving Errol Flynn, Olivia de Havilland, and Rosalind Russell provide good entertainment; the participants can't seem to make up their minds as to who loves whom.

GENTLEMAN JIM 1942 N/R, 104 MIN.

GENRE: DRAMA
DIRECTOR: RAOUL WALSH
CAST: ERROL FLYNN, ALAN HALE, JACK CARSON,
            ALEXIS SMITH, WARD BOND, WILLIAM FRAWLEY,
            RHYS WILLIAMS, MINOR WATSON, ARTHUR
            SHIELDS, JOHN LODER

This is the biography of boxing champ Jim Corbett who fought in the 1890s when boxing was not always considered an accepted sport. Errol Flynn plays the title role with understanding and a dash of comedy.

THE GREEN LIGHT 1937 N/R, 85 MIN.

GENRE: DRAMA
DIRECTOR: FRANK BORZAGE
CAST: ERROL FLYNN, ANITA LOUISE, MARGARET LINDSAY,
            CEDRIC HARDWICKE, HENRY O'NEILL, SPRING
            BYINGTON, ERIN O'BRIEN-MOORE, WALTER ABEL,
            HENRY KOLKER, PIERRE WATKIN

This is a philosophical drama about an idealist physician (Errol Flynn) who undergoes a conversion and leaves his profession to learn more about meaning in life.

HELLO GOD 1951 N/R, 64 MIN.

GENRE: DRAMA
DIRECTOR: WILLIAM MARSHALL
CAST: ERROL FLYNN, SHERRY JACKSON, WILLIAM
            MARSHALL, JOSEPH MAZZUCA, ARMANDO FORMICA

The film is of interest only because Flynn made it (in Italy) (1) in order to get out of his contract with Warner Bros. and (2) as a favor to his friend William Marshall. It also was controversial due to its pacifist nature, which was not in the public interest at that time. In fact, after Flynn made a new contract with Warners, he attempted to steal the negative. It was seldom shown—and then only in Europe. Flynn plays an unknown soldier who tells the stories of four soldiers killed during World War II and their feelings as they approach heaven.

HOLLYWOOD OUTTAKES 1984 N/R, 90 MIN.

GENRE: COMEDY
DIRECTOR: BRUCE GOLDSTEIN
CAST: HUMPHREY BOGART, BETTE DAVIS, ERROL FLYNN,
            GEORGE RAFT, JAMES CAGNEY, JUDY GARLAND,
            MICKEY ROONEY

This collection of bloopers and newsreel footage from the 1930s, 1940s and 1950s is terrific at times; at other times is just passable.

ISTANBUL 1957 N/R, 84 MIN.

GENRE: DRAMA
DIRECTOR: JOSEPH PEVNEY
CAST: ERROL FLYNN, CORNELL BORCHERS, JOHN
            BENTLEY, TORIN THATCHER, LEIF ERICKSON,
            NAT KING COLE

The highlight of this so-so film is Nat King Cole's rendition of "When I Fall in Love." The plot involves diamond smuggling in Istanbul and is a remake of 1947's Singapore.

IT'S A GREAT FEELING 1949 N/R, 84 MIN.

GENRE: MUSICAL/COMEDY
DIRECTOR: DAVID BUTLER
CAST: DENNIS MORGAN, DORIS DAY, JACK CARSON,
            BILL GOODWIN, GARY COOPER, JOAN CRAWFORD,
            ERROL FLYNN, DANNY KAYE, RONALD REAGAN,
            IRVING BACON, CLAIRE CARLETON, MEL BLANC,
            MICHAEL CURTIZ, DAVID BUTLER, FRANK CADY

This spoof on Hollywood musicals is Doris Day's third movie, and many Warner Bros. stars make cameo appearances. The story begins as Dennis Morgan and Jack Carson (Themselves) are preparing their next film and are unable to find a director, so Carson decides to take the job. Morgan is unhappy with Carson's decision and threatens to bow out—until Carson promises a waitress, Judy Adams (Day), at the Warner Bros. commissary a job as an actress if she will pose as his pregnant wife and convince Morgan that he needs the money. The ploy works, but there is no part for Judy in the film, and a dejected Judy returns to her Wisconsin home to marry her boyfriend. The film ends at the wedding when the newly married couple turns around, and the groom looks just like Errol Flynn (played by himself).

CAST

DENNIS MORGAN	HIMSELF
DORIS DAY	JUDY ADAMS
JACK CARSON	HIMSELF
BILL GOODWIN	ARTHUR TRENT
GARY COOPER	HIMSELF
JOAN CRAWFORD	HERSELF
ERROL FLYNN	JEFFREY BUSHDINKLE
DANNY KAYE	HIMSELF
RONALD REAGAN	HIMSELF
IRVING BACON	RR INFORMATION CLERK
CLAIRE CARLETON	GRACE
MEL BLANC	BUGS BUNNY (VOICE)
MICHAEL CURTIZ	HIMSELF
DAVID BUTLER	HIMSELF
FRANK CADY	OCULIST

KIM 1950 N/R, 112 MIN.

GENRE:	FAMILY/ADVENTURE/DRAMA
DIRECTOR:	VICTOR SAVILLE
CAST:	ERROL FLYNN, DEAN STOCKWELL, PAUL LUKAS, ROBERT DOUGLAS, THOMAS GOMEZ, CECIL KELLAWAY, REGINALD OWEN, ARNOLD MOSS, RICHARD HALE, HAYDEN RORKE, LAURETTE LUEZ, ROMAN TOPOROW, IVAN TRIESAULT, OLAF HYTTEN, HAMILTON CAMP

Based on the Rudyard Kipling story, this plot revolves around an orphaned boy, Kim (Dean Stockwell), who is recruited by the Secret Service in India and trained by Mahbub Ali (Errol Flynn) to become an espionage agent for the British. Kim's mission: work with Mahbub Ali and help rid India of the Czarist Russians who are causing trouble in India.

CAST

ERROL FLYNN	MAHBUB ALI, THE RED BEARD

DEAN STOCKWELL	KIM
PAUL LUKAS	LAMA
ROBERT DOUGLAS	COLONEL CREIGHTON
THOMAS GOMEZ	EMISSARY
CECIL KELLAWAY	HURREE CHUNDER
REGINALD OWEN	FATHER VICTOR
ARNOLD MOSS	LURGAN SAHIB
RICHARD HALE	HASSAN BEY, THE NARRATOR
HAYDEN RORKE	MAJOR AINSLEY
LAURETTE LUEZ	LALULI
ROMAN TOPOROW	RUSSIAN
IVAN TRIESAULT	RUSSIAN
OLAF HYTTEN	MR. HAIRLEE
HAMILTON CAMP	THORPE

KING'S RHAPSODY 1955 N/R, 93 MIN.

GENRE:	DRAMA/MUSICAL/ROMANCE
DIRECTOR:	HERBERT WILCOX
CAST:	ANNA NEAGLE, ERROL FLYNN, PATRICE WYMORE, MARTITA HUNT, FINLAY CURRIE, FRANCIS DE WOLFF, JOAN BENHAM, MILES MALLESON, REGINALD TATE, BRIAN FRANKLIN, EDMUND HOCKRIDGE

British actress icon Anna Neagle teams with Errol Flynn in this musical/drama based on Igor Novella's musical play. A prince (Flynn) falls in love with a commoner (Neagle) and decides to go into exile to be with his love. But, when his father, the King, dies, he returns to take the throne and the obligatory bride (Patrice Wymore—Flynn's wife at the time). When he is finally free, his true love rejects him, knowing his people need him more.

CAST

ANNA NEAGLE	MARTA KARILLOS
ERROL FLYNN	KING RICHARD
PATRICE WYMORE	PRINCESS CRISTIANE

MARTITA HUNT	QUEEN MOTHER
FINLAY CURRIE	KING PAUL
FRANCIS DE WOLFF	THE PRIME MINISTER
JOAN BENHAM	COUNTESS ASTRID
MILES MALLESON	JULES
REGINALD TATE	KING PETER
BRIAN FRANKLIN	BOY KING
EDMUND HOCKRIDGE	THE SERENADER (VOICE)

LILACS IN THE SPRING 1954 N/R, 94 MIN.

AKA:	LET'S MAKE UP
GENRE:	FAMILY/COMEDY/ROMANCE/FANTASY
DIRECTOR:	HERBERT WILCOX
CAST:	ANNA NEAGLE, ERROL FLYNN, DAVID FARRAR, KATHLEEN HARRISON, PETER GRAVES, HELEN HAYE, ALAN GIFFORD, GEORGE MARGO, SCOTT SANDERS, JENNIFER MITCHELL, SAM KYDD, STEPHEN BOYD, SEAN CONNERY

Following a head injury during a London air raid, Carole Beaumont (Anna Neagle) is knocked unconscious. She suffers identity problems while unconscious, and she seems to be King Charles' (David Farrar) courtesan Nell Gwyn (also played by Neagle). Later, while recovering at a country home, Carole loses consciousness again and appears to be Queen Victoria (also played by Neagle). Finally, Carole reprises her mother Lillian Grey's (also played by Neagle) life and is married to John Beaumont (Errol Flynn), who helps her find love and success on the stage.

CAST

ANNA NEAGLE	CAROLE/LILLIAN/NELL/QUEEN
ERROL FLYNN	JOHN "BEAU" BEAUMONT
DAVID FARRAR	CHARLES KING/KING CHARLES II
KATHLEEN HARRISON	KATE
PETER GRAVES	ALBERT GUTMAN/PRINCE ALBERT
HELEN HAYE	LADY DRAYTON

ALAN GIFFORD	HOLLYWOOD DIRECTOR
GEORGE MARGO	REPORTER
SCOTT SANDERS	OLD GEORGE
JENNIFER MITCHELL	YOUNG CAROLE
SAM KYDD	ACTOR
STEPHEN BOYD	BEAUMONT'S COMPANION

MARA MARU 1952 N/R, 98 MIN.

GENRE: ADVENTURE
DIRECTOR: GORDON DOUGLAS
CAST: ERROL FLYNN, RUTH ROMAN, RAYMOND BURR,
            RICHARD WEBB, NESTOR PAIVA, PAUL PICERNI,
            DAN SEYMOUR, GEORGES RENAVENT, MICHAEL
            ROSS, DON C. HARVEY

Salvage divers (Errol Flynn and Raymond Burr) vie for sunken treasure off the Philippines.

THE MASTER OF BALLANTRAE 1953 N/R, 88 MIN.

GENRE: ADVENTURE
DIRECTOR: WILLIAM KEIGHLEY
CAST: ERROL FLYNN, ROGER LIVESEY, ANTHONY STEEL,
            BEATRICE CAMPBELL, YVONNE FURNEAUX, FELIX
            AYLMER, MERVYN JOHNS, CHARLES GOLDNER,
            RALPH TRUMAN, FRANCIS DE WOLFF

This film is based (loosely) on Robert Louis Stevenson's story of the Scottish rebellion. Errol Flynn fights against the British monarchy—and his own brother (Anthony Steel) for the woman he loves.

MONTANA 1950 N/R, 77 MIN.

GENRE:	WESTERN/ACTION/ADVENTURE/ROMANCE
DIRECTOR:	RAY ENRIGHT
CAST:	ERROL FLYNN, ALEXIS SMITH, S. Z. SAKALL, DOUGLAS KENNEDY, JAMES BROWN, IAN MACDONALD, MONTE BLUE, CHARLES IRWIN, PAUL E. BURNS, LESTER MATTHEWS, TUDOR OWEN, LANE CHANDLER, DOROTHY ADAMS, CREIGHTON HALE, KERMIT MAYNARD

Morgan Lane (Errol Flynn) is an Australian sheepherder who arrives in the Montana territory where he plans to graze his sheep. But, cattle ranchers—including Maria Singleton (Alexis Smith) and Rodney Ackroyd (Douglas Kennedy)—are already there and lead the neighboring cattlemen against the intruders. Battles ensue. But, later, Morgan and Maria find time for love and agree that cattle ranchers and sheepherders are able to live together.

CAST

ERROL FLYNN	MORGAN LANE
ALEXIS SMITH	MARIA SINGLETON
S.Z. SAKALL	POPPA OTTO SCHULTZ
DOUGLAS KENNEDY	RODNEY ACKROYD
JAMES BROWN	TEX COYNE
IAN MACDONALD	SLIM REEVES
MONTE BLUE	CHARLIE PENROSE
CHARLES IRWIN	MACKENZIE
PAUL E. BURNS	TECUMSEH BURKE
LESTER MATTHEWS	GEORGE FORSYTHE
TUDOR OWEN	JACK
LANE CHANDLER	SHERIFF JAKE OVERBY
DOROTHY ADAMS	MRS. KITTY MAYNARD
CREIGHTON HALE	RANCHER
KERMIT MAYNARD	COWHAND

NEVER SAY GOODBYE 1946 N/R, 96 MIN.

GENRE: COMEDY
DIRECTOR: JAMES V. KERN
CAST: ERROL FLYNN, ELEANOR PARKER, LUCILE WATSON,
             S.Z. SAKALL, FORREST TUCKER, DONALD WOODS,
             PEGGY KNUDSEN, TOM D'ANDREA, HATTIE
             MCDANIEL, ARTHUR SHIELDS

After divorcing his wife, Eileen (Eleanor Parker), Philip Gayley (Errol Flynn) wants a second chance for happiness with her.

NORTHERN PURSUIT 1943 N/R, 93 MIN.

GENRE: ACTION/ADVENTURE/DRAMA/ROMANCE
DIRECTOR: RAOUL WALSH
CAST: ERROL FLYNN, JULIE BISHOP, HELMUT DANTINE,
             JOHN RIDGELY, GENE LOCKHART, TOM TULLY,
             MONTE BLUE, BERNARD NEDELL, ROSE HIGGINS,
             ALEC CRAIG

Canadian Mountie Steve Wagner (Errol Flynn) tracks down Nazi pilot Col. Hugo von Keller (Helmut Dantine) and, when he catches up with him, Wagner, whose parents were born in Germany, pretends to have sympathy for von Keller's cause. The ruse works, and von Keller leads Wagner to a Nazi hide-away where a plane is hidden. The plan is to use the plane to bomb North America. Will Wagner be able to stop the bombing plans and break up the espionage ring operating in Canada?

CAST

ERROL FLYNN	CORPORAL STEVE WAGNER
JULIE BISHOP	LAURA MCBAIN
HELMUT DANTINE	COLONEL HUGO VON KELLER
JOHN RIDGELY	JIM AUSTIN
GENE LOCKHART	ERNST
TOM TULLY	INSPECTOR BARNETT

MONTE BLUE	JEAN
BERNARD NEDELL	TOM DAGOR
ROSE HIGGINS	ROSE DAGOR
ALEC CRAIG	ANGUS MCBAIN

OBJECTIVE, BURMA! 1945 N/R, 142 MIN.

GENRE:	ACTION/DRAMA/ADVENTURE
DIRECTOR:	RAOUL WALSH
CAST:	ERROL FLYNN, WILLIAM PRINCE, JAMES BROWN, GEORGE TOBIAS, HENRY HULL, WARNER ANDERSON, JOHN ALVIN, MARK STEVENS, RICHARD ERDMAN, ANTHONY CARUSO, JOEL ALLEN, WILLIAM HUDSON, LESTER MATHEWS, GEORGE TYNE, RODD REDWING

Captain Nelson (Errol Flynn) is the leader of 50 World War II American paratroopers who land behind enemy lines in Burma with a mission: destroy a Japanese radar station. They complete the mission successfully, but then they are attacked and must fight their way on foot through 150 miles of the jungle to escape.

CAST

ERROL FLYNN	CAPTAIN NELSON
WILLIAM PRINCE	LIEUTENANT SID JACOBS
JAMES BROWN	STAFF SERGEANT TREACY
GEORGE TOBIAS	CORPORAL GABBY GORDON
HENRY HULL	MARK WILLIAMS
WARNER ANDERSON	COLONEL J. CARTER
JOHN ALVIN	HOGAN
MARK STEVENS	LIEUTENANT BARKER
RICHARD ERDMAN	PRIVATE NEBRASKA HOOPER
ANTHONY CARUSO	MIGGLEORI
JOEL ALLEN	CORPORAL BROPHY
WILLIAM HUDSON	FRED HOLLIS
LESTER MATHEWS	MAJOR FITZPATRICK
GEORGE TYNE	PRIVATE SOAPY HIGGINS

RODD REDWING   SERGEANT CHATTU

THE PERFECT SPECIMEN 1937 N/R, 97 MIN.

GENRE: COMEDY
DIRECTOR: MICHAEL CURTIZ
CAST: ERROL FLYNN, JOAN BLONDELL, HUGH HERBERT,
            EDWARD EVERETT HORTON, DICK FORAN, MAY
            ROBSON, BEVERLY ROBERTS, ALLEN JENKINS,
            DENNIE MOORE, HUGH O'CONNELL

A wealthy woman (May Robson) shelters her grandson (Errol Flynn) from the outside world until a beautiful woman (Joan Blondell) enters the picture, and the grandmother loses control.

THE PRINCE AND THE PAUPER 1937 N/R, 115 MIN.

GENRE: FAMILY/ADVENTURE/DRAMA/FANTASY
DIRECTOR: WILLIAM KEIGHLEY
CAST: ERROL FLYNN, CLAUDE RAINS, BILLY MAUCH,
            ROBERT J. MAUCH, ALAN HALE, MONTAGU LOVE,
            BARTON MACLANE, HENRY STEPHENSON, ERIC
            PORTMAN, HALLIWELL HOBBES, LIONEL PAPE,
            LEONARD WILLEY, MURRAY KINNELL, PHYLLIS
            BARRY, IVAN F. SIMPSON

Two boys meet—one is Prince Edward (Robert J. Mauch), and the other is a poor boy from London's slums, Tom (Billy Mauch)—and are struck by their physical resemblance to each other. While playing, they exchange clothes and identities, and Edward is evicted from the palace by the Captain of the Guard (Alan Hale), who believes he is a pauper. Now, Tom is thought to be the Prince of Wales by everyone except the evil Earl of Hertford (Claude Rains), who uses the deception as his chance to control the throne. Meanwhile, Edward lives with Tom's father (Barton MacLane) until he is befriended by a soldier of fortune, Miles Hendon (Errol Flynn), who takes him to the palace where he proves his real identity in time to be crowned King of England. A great musical score backs up this film version of Mark Twain's story.

CAST

ERROL FLYNN	MILES HENDON
CLAUDE RAINS	EARL OF HERTFORD
BILLY MAUCH	TOM CANTY
ROBERT J. MAUCH	PRINCE EDWARD
ALAN HALE	CAPTAIN OF THE GUARD
MONTAGU LOVE	HENRY VIII
BARTON MACLANE	JOHN CANTY
HENRY STEPHENSON	DUKE OF NORFOLK
ERIC PORTMAN	FIRST LORD
HALLIWELL HOBBES	ARCHBISHOP
LIONEL PAPE	SECOND LORD
LEONARD WILLEY	THIRD LORD
MURRAY KINNELL	HUGO
PHYLLIS BARRY	BARMAID
IVAN F. SIMPSON	CLEMENS

THE PRIVATE LIVES OF ELIZABETH AND ESSEX 1939 N/R, 106 MIN.

AKA:	ELIZABETH THE QUEEN
GENRE:	DRAMA/ROMANCE
DIRECTOR:	MICHAEL CURTIZ
CAST:	BETTE DAVIS, ERROL FLYNN, OLIVIA DE HAVILLAND, DONALD CRISP, NANETTE FABRAY, VINCENT PRICE, ALAN HALE, HENRY STEPHENSON, HENRY DANIELL, LEO G. CARROLL, JAMES STEPHENSON, RALPH FORBES, ROBERT WARWICK, JOHN SUTTON, GUY BELLIS

This 16th-century drama is VERY loosely based on the relationship of Queen Elizabeth I (Bette Davis) and the Earl of Essex (Errol Flynn). They endure a love/hate affair leading to the Earl's execution in the Tower of London.

CAST

BETTE DAVIS	QUEEN ELIZABETH
ERROL FLYNN	EARL OF ESSEX
OLIVIA DE HAVILLAND	LADY PENELOPE GRAY
DONALD CRISP	FRANCIS BACON
NANETTE FABRAY	MISTRESS MARGARET RADCLIFFE
VINCENT PRICE	SIR WALTER RALEIGH
ALAN HALE	EARL OF TYRONE
HENRY STEPHENSON	LORD BURGHLEY
HENRY DANIELL	SIR ROBERT CECIL
LEO G. CARROLL	SIR EDWARD COKE
JAMES STEPHENSON	SIR THOMAS EGERTON
RALPH FORBES	LORD KNOLLYS
ROBERT WARWICK	LORD MOUNTJOY
JOHN SUTTON	CAPT. ARMAND
GUY BELLIS	LORD CHARLES HOWARD

ROCKY MOUNTAIN 1950 N/R, 83 MIN.

GENRE:	WESTERN/ACTION/ADVENTURE
DIRECTOR:	WILLIAM KEIGHLEY
CAST:	ERROL FLYNN, PATRICE WYMORE, SCOTT FORBES, GUINN "BIG BOY" WILLIAMS, SLIM PICKENS, SHEB WOOLEY, YAKIMA CANUTT, DICKIE JONES, HOWARD PETRIE, CHUBBY JOHNSON, ROBERT "BUZZ" HENRY, PETER COE, RUSH WILLIAMS, MARIANNE STONE, ALEX SHARP

While a band of Confederate soldiers, led by Captain Lave Barstow (Errol Flynn), is in California trying to recruit soldiers, they rescue Johanna (Patrice Wymore) who is aboard a stage coach that is being attacked by Indians. Johanna is the fiancée of Union soldier Lt. Rickey (Scott Forbes), and Barstow uses her as the bait to lure Rickey and his patrol of Union soldiers into battle. They capture the Union soldiers, but the Indians launch their own attack, and Barstow allows the Union soldiers and Johanna to escape the Indian massacre.

CAST

Errol Flynn	Capt. Lave Barstow
Patrice Wymore	Johanna Carter
Scott Forbes	Lt. Rickey
Guinn "Big Boy" Williams	Pap Dennison
Slim Pickens	Plank
Sheb Wooley	Kay Rawlins
Yakima Canutt	Trooper Ryan
Dickie Jones	Jim (Buck) Wheat
Howard Petrie	Cole Smith/California Beal
Chubby Johnson	Gil Craigie
Robert "Buzz" Henry	Kip Waterson
Peter Coe	Pierre Duchesne
Rush Williams	Jonas Wetherby
Marianne Stone	Stage Passenger
Alex Sharp	Barnes

THE ROOTS OF HEAVEN 1958 N/R, 131 MIN.

GENRE: DRAMA
DIRECTOR: JOHN HUSTON
CAST: ERROL FLYNN, TREVOR HOWARD, JULIETTE GRECO,
           EDDIE ALBERT, ORSON WELLES, PAUL LUKAS,
           HERBERT LOM, GREGOIRE ASLAN, ANDRE LUGUET,
           FRIEDRICH VON LEDEBUR

A group of white adventurers in Africa become involved in saving the elephants.

SAN ANTONIO 1945 N/R, 110 MIN.

GENRE: WESTERN/ROMANCE
DIRECTOR: DAVID BUTLER
CAST: ERROL FLYNN, ALEXIS SMITH, S. Z. SAKALL,
           VICTOR FRANCEN, FLORENCE BATES, JOHN LITEL,
           PAUL KELLY, MONTE BLUE, DOODLES WEAVER,

PAUL KELLY, ROBERT SHAYNE, JOHN ALVIN, ROBERT BARRAT, PEDRO DE CORDOBA, TOM TYLER

Cattleman Clay Hardin (Errol Flynn) arrives in San Antonio, Texas, to capture Roy Stuart (Paul Kelly) whom he believes leads a cattle rustling gang. Upon arrival, Clay is attracted to dance-hall singer Jeanne Starr (Alexis Smith) who works in the saloon owned by Roy. Clay believes that Jeanne is in with the crooked rustlers, but he falls in love with her. Tensions rise after Clay's friend Charlie Bell (John Litel) is murdered and culminate in a shoot-out at the Alamo.

CAST

ERROL FLYNN	CLAY HARDIN
ALEXIS SMITH	JEANNE STARR
S. Z. SAKALL	SACHA BOZIC
VICTOR FRANCEN	LEGARE
FLORENCE BATES	HENRIETTA
JOHN LITEL	CHARLIE BELL
PAUL KELLY	ROY STUART
MONTE BLUE	CLEVE ANDREWS
DOODLES WEAVER	SQUARE-DANCE CALLER
PAUL KELLY	ROY STUART
ROBERT SHAYNE	CAPT. MORGAN
JOHN ALVIN	PONY SMITH
ROBERT BARRAT	COL. JOHNSON
PEDRO DE CORDOBA	RICARDO TORREON
TOM TYLER	LAFE MCWILLIAMS

THE SANTA FE TRAIL 1940 N/R, 110 MIN.

GENRE:	WESTERN/ADVENTURE/ACTION/DRAMA/ROMANCE
DIRECTOR:	MICHAEL CURTIZ
CAST:	ERROL FLYNN, OLIVIA DE HAVILLAND, RAYMOND MASSEY, RONALD REAGAN, ALAN HALE, WILLIAM LUNDIGAN, VAN HEFLIN, GENE REYNOLDS, HENRY O'NEILL, WARD BOND, GUINN "BIG BOY" WILLIAMS, ALAN BAXTER, MORONI OLSEN,

DAVID BRUCE, JOHN LITEL

In 1854, just before graduating from West Point, cadets Jeb Stuart (Errol Flynn) and George Armstrong Custer (Ronald Reagan) are given a dangerous assignment of reporting to Fort Leavenworth, Kansas, to confront abolitionist John Brown (Raymond Massey), who is using his own unique methods to free the slaves. While a cat-and-mouse game ensues, Stuart and Custer seek the affection of Kit Carson Halliday (Olivia de Havilland).

CAST

ERROL FLYNN	JEB STUART
OLIVIA DE HAVILLAND	KIT CARSON HOLLIDAY
RAYMOND MASSEY	JOHN BROWN
RONALD REAGAN	GEORGE ARMSTRONG CUSTER
ALAN HALE	TEX BELL
WILLIAM LUNDIGAN	BOB HOLLIDAY
VAN HEFLIN	CARL RADER
GENE REYNOLDS	JASON BROWN
HENRY O'NEILL	CYRUS K. HOLLIDAY
WARD BOND	TOWNLEY
GUINN "BIG BOY" WILLIAMS	WINDY BRODY
ALAN BAXTER	OLIVER BROWN
MORONI OLSEN	COLONEL ROBERT E. LEE
DAVID BRUCE	PHIL SHERIDAN
JOHN LITEL	MARTIN

THE SEA HAWK 1940 N/R, 124 MIN.

GENRE:	ACTION/ADVENTURE/ROMANCE
DIRECTOR:	MICHAEL CURTIZ
CAST:	ERROL FLYNN, BRENDA MARSHALL, CLAUDE RAINS, FLORA ROBSON, ALAN HALE, DONALD CRISP, GILBERT ROLAND, WILLIAM LUNDIGAN, MONTAGU LOVE, FRANCIS McDONALD, HENRY DANIELL, UNA O'CONNOR, JAMES STEPHENSON, JULIEN MITCHELL, J.M. KERRIGAN

Errol Flynn is definitely at his swashbuckling best as 1850s British pirate Geoffrey Thorpe leads the Sea Hawk pirates on raids and captures more than 50 Spanish ships. In the process, he learns that the Spanish are planning to attack England and have placed spies in Queen Elizabeth's (Flora Robson) court. But, Elizabeth does not approve of Thorpe's pirating tactics and demands that he change his ways. Meanwhile, Thorpe falls in love with Dona Maria (Brenda Marshall), and now he must expose the treachery to save his country and win the love of Dona Maria.

CAST

ERROL FLYNN	GEOFFREY THORPE
BRENDA MARSHALL	DONA MARIA
CLAUDE RAINS	DON JOSE ALVAREZ DE CORDOBA
FLORA ROBSON	QUEEN ELEZABETH
ALAN HALE	CARL PITT
DONALD CRISP	SIR JOHN BURLESON
GILBERT ROLAND	CAPTAIN LOPEZ
WILLIAM LUNDIGAN	DANNY LOGAN
MONTAGU LOVE	KING PHILLLIP II
FRANCIS MCDONALD	KRONER
HENRY DANIELL	LORD WOLFINGHAM
UNA O'CONNOR	MISS LATHAM
JAMES STEPHENSON	ABBOTT
JULIEN MITCHELL	OLIVER SCOTT
J.M. KERRIGAN	ELI MATSON

SILVER RIVER 1948 N/R, 108 MIN.

GENRE: WESTERN/DRAMA/ROMANCE
DIRECTOR: RAOUL WALSH
CAST: ERROL FLYNN, ANN SHERIDAN, THOMAS MITCHELL, BRUCE BENNETT, TOM D'ANDREA, BARTON MACLANE, MONTE BLUE, JONATHAN HALE, AL BRIDGE, ARTHUR SPACE, ART BAKER, JOSEPH E. BERNARD, JOSEPH CREHAN, PHILO MCCULLOUGH, IAN WOLFE

Mike McComb (Errol Flynn) is court martialed during the Civil War, and heads West with his friend "Pistol" Porter (Tom D'Andrea). Mike becomes a riverboat gambler and heads to Silver City, Nevada, where he plans to open his own gambling house. He makes a deal with Stanley Moore (Bruce Bennett) to become his partner in a silver mine and, in the process, tries to take Stanley's wife away from him. Many problems ensue, and President U.S. Grant (Joseph Crehan) even becomes involved.

CAST

ERROL FLYNN	"MIKE" McCOMB
ANN SHERIDAN	GEORGIA MOORE
THOMAS MITCHELL	JOHN PLATO BECK
BRUCE BENNETT	STANLEY MOORE
TOM D'ANDREA	"PISTOL" PORTER
BARTON MacLANE	"BANJO" SWEENEY
MONTE BLUE	"BUCK" CHEVIGEE
JONATHAN HALE	MAJOR SPENCER
AL BRIDGE	SLADE
ARTHUR SPACE	MAJOR ROSS
ART BAKER	MAJOR WILSON
JOSEPH E. BERNARD	RIVERBOAT CAPTAIN
JOSEPH CREHAN	PRESIDENT U.S. GRANT
PHILO McCULLOUGH	TRACY
IAN WOLFE	KANSAS PROCESS SERVER

THE SISTERS 1938 N/R, 95 MIN.

GENRE:	DRAMA
DIRECTOR:	ANATOLE LITVAK
CAST:	ERROL FLYNN, BETTE DAVIS, ANITA LOUISE, IAN HUNTER, DONALD CRISP, BEULAH BONDI, ALAN HALE, HENRY TRAVERS, JANE BRYAN, DICK FORAN, PATRIC KNOWLES, LEE PATRICK, LAURA HOPE CREWS, JANET SHAW, HARRY DAVENPORT

Three sisters, Louise (Bette Davis), Helen (Anita Louise), and Grace (Jane Bryan), find love and marriage in this drama set during the turn of the 20th century in San Francisco.

CAST

ERROL FLYNN	FRANK MEDLIN
BETTE DAVIS	LOUISE ELLIOTT MEDLIN
ANITA LOUISE	HELEN ELLIOTT JOHNSON
IAN HUNTER	WILLIAM BENSON
DONALD CRISP	TIM HAZELTON
BEULAH BONDI	ROSE ELLIOTT
ALAN HALE	SAM JOHNSON
HENRY TRAVERS	NED ELLIOTT
JANE BRYAN	GRACE ELLIOTT KNIVEL
DICK FORAN	TOM KNIVEL
PATRIC KNOWLES	NORMAN FRENCH
LEE PATRICK	FLORA GIBBON
LAURA HOPE CREWS	FLORA'S MOTHER
JANET SHAW	STELLA JOHNSON
HARRY DAVENPORT	DOC MOORE

THE SUN ALSO RISES 1957 N/R, 129 MIN.

GENRE:	DRAMA
DIRECTOR:	HENRY KING
CAST:	TYRONE POWER, AVA GARDNER, MEL FERRER, ERROL FLYNN, EDDIE ALBERT, GREGORY RATOFF, MARCEL DALIO, ROBERT EVANS, EDUARDO NORIEGA, HENRY DANIELL, JULIETTE GRECO, BOB CUNNINGHAM, DANIK PATISSON, JACQUELINE EVANS, CARLOS DAVID ORTIGOS

This rendition of Hemingway's classic story is about the "Lost Generation" of expatriates who roamed Europe between the two World Wars. The plot revolves around American news correspondent Jake Barnes (Tyrone Power), who suffers from impotence following the war. For a diversion, he travels to Spain with his cohorts—Mike

Campbell (Errol Flynn), Lady Brett Ashley (Ava Gardner), Robert Cohn (Mel Ferrer), and Bill Gorton (Eddie Albert). Lady Brett is engaged to Mike but is attracted to Jake, and, despite his impotence, she pursues him. While in Spain, Lady Brett becomes involved with matador Pedro Romero (Robert Evans), and adds one more man to her list of lovers.

CAST

TYRONE POWER	JACOB "JAKE" BARNES
AVA GARDNER	LADY BRETT ASHLEY
MEL FERRER	ROBERT COHN
ERROL FLYNN	MIKE CAMPBELL
EDDIE ALBERT	BILL GORTON
GREGORY RATOFF	COUNT MIPPIPOPOLOUS
MARCEL DALIO	ZIZI
ROBERT EVANS	PEDRO ROMERO
EDUARDO NORIEGA	JUANITO MONTOYA
HENRY DANIELL	ARMY DOCTOR
JULIETTE GRECO	GEORGETTE AUBIN
BOB CUNNINGHAM	HARRIS
DANIK PATISSON	MARIE
JACQUELINE EVANS	MRS. BRADDOCK
CARLOS DAVID ORTIGOS	ROMERO'S BROTHER

THANK YOUR LUCKY STARS 1943 N/R, 127 MIN.

GENRE:	MUSICAL/COMEDY
DIRECTOR:	DAVID BUTLER
CAST:	EDDIE CANTOR, DINAH SHORE, BETTE DAVIS, HUMPHREY BOGART, OLIVIA DE HAVILLAND, IDA LUPINO, ERROL FLYNN, JOHN GARFIELD, DENNIS MORGAN, S. Z. SAKALL, JOAN LESLIE, ANN SHERIDAN, HATTIE MCDANIEL, EDWARD EVERETT HORTON, JACK CARSON

Movie star Eddie Cantor (Himself) steps in as chairman of the Cavalcade of Stars benefit show and creates so many problems that the producers (S. Z. Sakall and Edward Everett Horton) arrange to have him kidnapped. They plan to replace him with his look-a-like, talented bus driver Joe Simpson (also Eddie Cantor), who has been looking for work as an actor but can't get a job because he looks so much like Cantor. Simpson proves to be a hit and is signed to a film contract.

CAST

EDDIE CANTOR	HIMSELF/JOE SIMPSON
DINAH SHORE	HERSELF
BETTE DAVIS	HERSELF
HUMPHREY BOGART	HIMSELF
OLIVIA DE HAVILLAND	HERSELF
IDA LUPINO	HERSELF
ERROL FLYNN	HIMSELF
JOHN GARFIELD	HIMSELF
DENNIS MORGAN	TOMMY RANDOLPH
S. Z. SAKALL	DR. SCHLENNA
JOAN LESLIE	PAT DIXON
ANN SHERIDAN	HERSELF
HATTIE McDANIEL	GOSSIP
EDWARD EVERETT HORTON	FARNSWORTH
JACK CARSON	HIMSELF

THAT FORSYTE WOMAN 1949 N/R, 112 MIN.

GENRE:	DRAMA
DIRECTOR:	COMPTON BENNETT
CAST:	ERROL FLYNN, GREER GARSON, WALTER PIDGEON, ROBERT YOUNG, JANET LEIGH, HARRY DAVENPORT, HALLIWELL HOBBES, STANLEY LOGAN, LUMSDEN HARE, AUBREY MATHER

Based on John Galsworthy's novel, *The Man of Property*, from *The Forsyte Saga*, Soames Forsyte's (Errol Flynn) marriage goes on the rocks, and the split has repercussions that echo throughout the family.

THEY DIED WITH THEIR BOOTS ON 1941 N/R, 140 MIN.

GENRE: WESTERN
DIRECTOR: RAOUL WALSH
CAST: ERROL FLYNN, OLIVIA DE HAVILLAND,
            ARTHUR KENNEDY, WALTER HAMPDEN,
            SYDNEY GREENSTREET, GENE LOCKHART,
            ANTHONY QUINN, CHARLEY GRAPEWIN,
            HATTIE McDANIEL, REGIS TOOMEY,
            EDDIE ACUFF

This biography covers the life of George Custer (Errol Flynn), from his days as a West Point cadet, through Civil War service, to Indian fighting in America's West.

TOO MUCH, TOO SOON 1958 N/R, 122 MIN.

GENRE: DRAMA
DIRECTOR: ART NAPOLEON
CAST: DOROTHY MALONE, ERROL FLYNN, EFREM
            ZIMBALIST, JR., RAY DANTON, NEVA PATTERSON,
            MURRAY HAMILTON, MARTIN MILNER, JOHN
            DENNIS, ED KEMMER, ROBERT ELLENSTEIN

This is the biography of John Barrymore's (Errol Flynn) actress daughter, Diana (Dorothy Malone), whose self-destructive behavior brought her to a tragic end.

UNCERTAIN GLORY 1944 N/R, 102 MIN.

GENRE: DRAMA/THRILLER/ROMANCE
DIRECTOR: RAOUL WALSH
CAST: ERROL FLYNN, PAUL LUKAS, JEAN SULLIVAN,
            LUCILE WATSON, FAYE EMERSON, DOUGLASS
            DUMBRILLE, DENNIS HOEY, SHELDON LEONARD,
            ODETTE MYRTIL, FRANCIS PIERLOT, JAMES FLAVIN,

CONNIE LEON, CARL HARBAUGH, JOYCE TUCKER,
ART SMITH

During World War II, Jean Picard (Errol Flynn) is a Frenchman
destined for the guillotine when the prison is bombed by the R.A.F.
He escapes, heads for Spain, and is pursued by detective Marcel
Bonet (Paul Lucas) who recaptures him. On their return, they are
delayed in a small village where Jean meets Marianne (Jean Sullivan)
and falls for her. While searching for resistance saboteurs, the Nazis
capture French hostages and threaten their deaths if the saboteur
does not reveal himself. Jean poses as the saboteur and sacrifices
himself to save Marianne and the other hostages and, in the process,
help the cause of the Allies.

CAST

ERROL FLYNN	JEAN PICARD
PAUL LUKAS	INSPECTOR MARCEL BONET
JEAN SULLIVAN	MARIANNE
LUCILE WATSON	MME. MARET
FAYE EMERSON	LOUISE
DOUGLASS DUMBRILLE	POLICE COMMISSIONER LaFARGE
DENNIS HOEY	FATHER LE CLERC
SHELDON LEONARD	HENRI DUVAL
ODETTE MYRTIL	MME. BONET
FRANCIS PIERLOT	FATHER LA BORDE
JAMES FLAVIN	CAPTAIN OF MOBILE GUARD
CONNIE LEON	BONET'S MAID
CARL HARBAUGH	INNKEEPER
JOYCE TUCKER	MICHELE BONET
ART SMITH	WARDEN

VIRGINIA CITY 1940 N/R, 125 MIN.

GENRE:	WESTERN/ACTION/DRAMA/ROMANCE
DIRECTOR:	MICHAEL CURTIZ
CAST:	ERROL FLYNN, MIRIAM HOPKINS, RANDOLPH SCOTT, HUMPHREY BOGART, JOHN LITEL,

ALAN HALE, FRANK MCHUGH, DOUGLASS
DUMBRILLE, GUINN "BIG BOY" WILLIAMS,
MORONI OLSEN, RUSSELL HICKS, DICKIE JONES,
FRANK WILCOX, RUSSELL SIMPSON, VICTOR KILIAN

After Union officer Capt. Kerry Bradford (Errol Flynn) escapes from a Confederate prison, he heads to Nevada. There he learns that the Confederate Prison boss, Capt. Vance Irby (Randolph Scott), is planning to send a large shipment of gold to Confederate forces to prolong the war. Bradford intends to make sure that doesn't happen. Also seeking the gold is Mexican outlaw Murrell (Humphrey Bogart), and problems ensue.

CAST

ERROL FLYNN	CAPT. KERRY BRADFORD
MIRIAM HOPKINS	JULIA HAYNE
RANDOLPH SCOTT	CAPT. VANCE IRBY
HUMPHREY BOGART	JOHN MURRELL
JOHN LITEL	THOMAS MARSHALL
ALAN HALE	OLAF "MOOSE" SWENSON
FRANK MCHUGH	MR. UPJOHN
DOUGLASS DUMBRILLE	MAJ. DREWERY
GUINN "BIG BOY" WILLIAMS	"MARBLEHEAD"
MORONI OLSEN	DR. ROBERT CAMERON
RUSSELL HICKS	JOHN ARMISTEAD
DICKIE JONES	COBBY GILL
FRANK WILCOX	UNION OUTPOST SOLDIER
RUSSELL SIMPSON	FRANK GAYLORD
VICTOR KILIAN	ABRAHAM LINCOLN

"I've had a hell of a lot of fun and I've enjoyed every minute of it."

Index

About the Author

Jim Turiello grew up in Washington Heights, New York, where his favorite pastimes were playing football, baseball, basketball and bowling. In his spare time he went to the many movie palaces in his neighborhood, as well as, movie houses in Times Square, New York.

He claims to have seen *The Adventures of Robin Hood* over 100 times and most of Errol Flynn's movies close to that amount. He has added *The Godfather I & II* and the original *King Kong* to his list of movies-I-never-get-tired-of-watching. An avid football fan of the San Diego Chargers, Jim writes a weekly sports column for BrianSmithRadio.com. Since the 80's he has been a regular on numerous sports radio shows in the tri-state area. As a prolific writer his contributions to music, movie and collectable magazines are too numerous to mention. Jim produced a unique trading card set, The James Dean Collection, that included 50 photos of Dean with an original biographical story that ran on the reverse of each card. The card set received rave reviews when it was released and is still available at the James Dean Gallery in Fairmount, Indiana, James Dean's hometown.

He loves to travel and has been to most Caribbean islands. He has two daughters and four sons, two of his sons are pursuing careers in the movie business. Jim lives with his soul mate, Ebie, who shares a birthday with Errol Flynn.

CPSIA information can be obtained at www.ICGtesting.com
Printed in the USA
BVOW011344220712

295813BV00006B/22/P